THE 7 Secrets OF SYNCHRONICITY

THE
7 Secrets OF
SYNCHRONICITY

Your Guide to Finding Meaning in Signs Big and Small

TRISH MACGREGOR
& ROB MACGREGOR

HAY HOUSE
Australia • Canada • Hong Kong • India
South Africa • United Kingdom • United States

First published in the United States by Adams Media, a division of F+W Media, Inc.
57 Littlefield Street, Avon, MA 02322. U.S.A. *www.adamsmedia.com*

First published and distributed in the United Kingdom by:
Hay House UK Ltd, 292B Kensal Rd, London W10 5BE. Tel.: (44) 20 8962 1230; Fax: (44)
20 8962 1239. www.hayhouse.co.uk

Published and distributed in Australia by:
Hay House Australia Ltd, 18/36 Ralph St, Alexandria NSW 2015. Tel.: (61) 2 9669 4299;
Fax: (61) 2 9669 4144. www.hayhouse.com.au

Published and distributed in the Republic of South Africa by:
Hay House SA (Pty), Ltd, PO Box 990, Witkoppen 2068. Tel./Fax: (27) 11 467 8904.
www.hayhouse.co.za

Published and distributed in India by:
Hay House Publishers India, Muskaan Complex, Plot No.3, B-2, Vasant Kunj, New Delhi –
110 070. Tel.: (91) 11 4176 1620; Fax: (91) 11 4176 1630. www.hayhouse.co.in

A catalogue record for this book is available from the British Library.

ISBN 978-1-8485-0292-5

Printed and bound in Great Britain by
CPI Mackays, Chatham ME5 8TD

MIX
Paper from
responsible sources
FSC® C020471

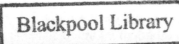

This one is for Megan with love always.

ACKNOWLEDGMENTS

No book is written in a vacuum. We owe our deepest thanks to all of you who visited our blog, who contributed stories to this book, and whose insights into the mystery of synchronicity have broadened our knowledge.

Thanks also to our agent, Al Zuckerman, who went through the book with a Virgo's attention to detail, and to Pisces Paula Munier, who saw the larger picture.

CONTENTS

PART TWO

The Magic

INTRODUCTION

In early February 2009, we started a blog on synchronicity as a research tool and to gather stories for this book. It was our first experience at blogging and we weren't sure how the process worked or what the response would be. We posted several personal stories about meaningful coincidences and invited readers to contribute their own.

At the end of our first week, we had gotten thirty-eight hits, mostly from friends and family, but hadn't received a single story. Apparently, with more than 100 million blogs on the Internet we had to find a way to spread the word that our blog even existed. So we set up a Google alert for the term "synchronicity" and every day, dozens of links to blogs and websites that mentioned the word crowded our inbox. We sifted through them, searching for dramatic stories about synchronicity, and invited people to send us their stories. Several weeks before our blog's year anniversary, the hits had soared to nearly 50,000 and we had collected hundreds of stories. We were surprised not only by the extent of interest but by the willingness of readers to contribute and to allow us to use their stories in the book.

Even though synchronicities have been part of our lives for years, our own experiences multiplied fast and furiously during the research and writing of this book. It's as if our focus on the topic attracted the experiences, making it clear that we couldn't write the book as just "outside" observers of synchronicity. We had to be "inside" activists.

One evening, for example, Rob was editing a synchronicity story that included these lines:

"Good atmosphere, good friends, good conversation, good wine, good books, and the space between."

He paused a moment as he read the last phrase —the space between—then continued his editing. The next morning, he opened F. David Peat's autobiography, *Pathways of Chance*, to the place where the author was talking about his friendship with physicist David Bohm. The first thing Rob read was:

"Independent of our meetings and discussions I had been thinking about what I called *the space between*. It was an idea that could be applied in many areas, particularly to describe what happens when you look at art or read a work of literature. It is the space that lies between the observer and the observed; it is the space of the creative act that brings a poem or painting to life." And it's the space where synchronicities are born.

Another synchronicity quickly followed when a friend dropped by to advise us about a home repair. A leak had developed in our living room ceiling that we believed was a delayed result of roof damage from Hurricane Wilma, which hit our area in October 2005. Our friend, who is experienced in both insurance and the construction industry, remarked that if we intended for our homeowner's insurance to cover the repair, we would have to prove the leak was related to the hurricane.

Trish had stepped outside to get the mail and returned waving a flyer from a roofing company. It featured an offer for a free roof inspection. "If your roof has wind damage from Hurricane Wilma, we can assist you in documenting your claim to get the necessary monies to replace the roof" it promised. Although we never pursued the offer, the flyer had arrived precisely as we were talking about the roof damage—it even mentioned the hurricane from four years earlier.

The World of Synchronicity

The world of synchronicity shares some eerie parallels to the popular TV series *Lost*. In the series, a plane crashes on a deserted island and the survivors are confronted with all kinds of strange events, insights, and synchronistic connections to each other from the past. Nothing is what it appears. As the characters struggle to survive by organizing themselves as a community, their frailties and strengths as individuals reveal layered depths to their personalities that complicate next week's plot. Viewers are left with a sense of wonder, intrigue, and five million questions. Synchronicity is a lot like that—a magical adventure that expands our concepts of what is possible.

For us, this adventure began on December 12, 1981. It was our first date and Trish asked Rob if he'd ever heard of synchronicity. He had, and from that moment our lives were changed.

Fast forward to 1984. We were married and had quit our day jobs to pursue writing full time. We spent part of our time writing travel articles, and had joined a group of travel agents on a familiarization or "fam" trip. Even though our destination, Nashville, wasn't exactly our idea of a primo travel spot, the trip was free and we were open to anything.

Halfway through the flight, the air conditioning in our small commuter jet quit and the cabin quickly heated up. We grew uncomfortable, annoyed, and hungry. The man sitting next to us started talking about the travails of air travel, and pretty soon we were commiserating like thieves. We discovered that the man, whose name was German, had been born and raised in Latin America, like Trish. His family owned numerous hotels throughout Columbia; he owned a travel agency in Miami, and had connections within Avianca Airlines.

At the time, American tourists tended to avoid Colombia and Peru because of the rampant drug trade. Avianca was searching for innovative ways to encourage more tourism in those areas. German thought Avianca might be interested in providing free air passage to travel writers. He could arrange for accommodations, and in return, the writers would publish travel articles about Colombia and Peru. We would be in charge of finding the writers, leading the tours, and collecting the articles as they were published and sending them to Avianca. Would something like this interest us?

Thanks to the fortuitous synchronicity of sitting next to German on the plane, we began leading adventure tours to South America. We made several trips on a riverboat in the Upper Amazon and led numerous trips to destinations in Latin America. All of them provided fodder for novels as well as for travel and nonfiction articles.

Because of synchronicity, we felt we were on a roll. In September 1984, Trish sold her first novel, *In Shadow*, and Rob landed a ghostwriting project for the CEO of a Washington-based company, a contact we had made through writing magazine articles. A year later, Rob sold his first novel, *Crystal Skull*. We never returned to our day jobs. During the twenty-six years of our marriage, we've written sixty books, both fiction and nonfiction. We've gone wherever the synchronicities have led us.

Many times we talked about writing a book about synchronicity, but we didn't know how to do it, what approach to take, or where to start. Carl Jung seemed the logical place to begin, considering he had coined the term. But over the years, other projects took up our time, and we always put the synchronicity book on hold. Yet, our synchronicities multiplied.

One night in January 2009, we started playing around with the idea again. We were interested in anecdotes, the stories that illustrated the magic and mystery of synchronicity. Even so, we had trouble finding a theme. A day or two later, we realized that after all these years of experiencing synchronicities we were aware of certain concepts about the nature of "meaningful coincidence" that weren't widely known or understood.

Those concepts became the secrets, which we discuss in Part I. Although the secrets reveal a great deal about the phenomenon, we also felt there is an active magical element in which human beings can engage synchronicity and direct it for their own purposes. That magic became the subject of Part II of this book.

Technology—the Internet, blogs, e-mail— facilitated our research and made it possible to collect synchronicities from all over the world. Apparently we weren't ready to write the book until the technology existed that would allow us to make new contacts and gather stories from people around the world.

But What Does It Mean?

A synchronicity can simply serve to attune your awareness, to remind you that beneath the surface of daily life there's an underlying reality and unity that may not be immediately obvious. A synchronicity can serve as guidance, warning, affirmation, creative inspiration, and/or as evidence of individuation and psychological growth. It can offer a glimpse into your future, and cause you to feel you're on the right track, in the groove, exactly where you're supposed to be. All synchronicities, even the darker ones that caution us, have a mysterious quality.

This book will guide you toward becoming more aware of synchronicity. It will help you to decipher synchronicity's sometimes cryptic message, and to engage its power for transformation, so that you can improve your life and well-being. It does this by presenting stories and synchronicity practices that will enable you to make associations and interpret metaphors and symbols. In other words, the material in this book helps you to mine your own unconscious for answers.

With that in mind, dive into the secrets and embrace the synchronicities that begin to flow into your life. As Jean Shinoda Bolen noted in *The Tao of Psychology: Synchronicity and the Self*, "Synchronicity holds the promise that if we will change within, the patterns in our outer life will change also."

Part One
The Secrets

PART ONE

The Secrets

Secret 1

THE KNOWING

The first secret shows us that once we recognize coincidence as meaningful, we open ourselves to new information, new possibilities, new belief systems.

Synchronicity: the coming together of inner and outer events in a way that can't be explained by cause and effect and that is meaningful to the observer.

We live in uncertain times, where the tectonic plates of what we've taken for granted are shifting and our belief systems are in violent flux. But such turbulence presents many opportunities to grow and flourish as individuals, and "meaningful coincidences" or synchronicities certainly provide fertile ground for doing exactly that.

The first step is to recognize coincidences when they occur and consider the possibility that they might be meaningful. If you overlook or simply shrug off coincidences as insignificant, you miss opportunities to gain new understanding or a fresh look at some aspect of your life. Let's say, for example, that you haven't thought about an old college friend in years but run across that person's photo while cleaning out your closet. Later that day, you receive a friend request on Facebook from that individual. The message? Perhaps you should renew the friendship. The larger message? We are all connected at a deeper level.

The following list includes some typical kinds of synchronicities many people experience. Which ones have you experienced? How did you react? Did you dismiss the incident as an interesting but random coincidence? Did you act on it?

1. You read and research something you want—a certain kind of car, for instance, or a particular breed of dog. Suddenly you start seeing the car on the street, in driveways, or in parking lots, or you spot people walking that very breed of dog. At first, you think it might be a matter of awareness. You just never noticed before you took an interest. But then perhaps you walk out to your car in a parking lot and discover that the car of your dreams is parked next to you, and there's another one just like it on the other side of your car, too. Or, someone mentions that a friend has to get rid of his dog, and it's the very

breed that you want. Now it's more than awareness. It's synchronicity.

2. Over a short period of time, a name keeps recurring. It seems that everyone you run into has this name—your dentist, the cashier at the supermarket, a neighbor. Within a matter of hours or days, you meet someone new, and he or she has that name.

3. While on a trip, you see a house that captivates you. Every time you return to this neighborhood, you drive past the house and wonder about the person who lives there. Then on a flight, you strike up a conversation with a fellow passenger and discover he owns the house you have admired for so long.

4. You dream about a particular incident, then something nearly identical happens several days later.

5. You have a hunch to take a different route to work, only to discover that a car accident occurred on your usual route. You realize you would have been delayed for hours or perhaps been involved in the accident.

6. You have an idea for a story, novel, invention, product, or service that you believe is unique. Then you find out that two other people independently came up with the same idea, and beat you to it.

7. When you look at a clock, a microwave, or the time on your computer, even the digital readout on your treadmill, it seems the same numbers—maybe 1:11 or 9:11— keep popping up. It's as if you're being stalked by these numbers.

8. While thinking or talking about a particular bird, say a crow, a flock flies overhead. Or perhaps you're thinking about a particular book while browsing the aisles in a bookstore, and that book slips off the shelf and lands at

your feet. Or you randomly open a book and read a line that precisely addresses a question on your mind.

9. You lose an object and it "returns" to you in a way that defies the odds.

10. You feel discouraged about a relationship, your job, your finances, and you're about to give up. Then something unexpected occurs that makes you realize things aren't as dire as you thought.

In each example, synchronicity is at work and it's up to you to decipher the message. That is exactly what Swiss psychiatrist Carl Jung did when he first encountered a meaningful coincidence.

Experiencing Synchronicity

Jung was treating a young female patient, who related a dream in which she was given a golden scarab. He knew the scarab was a symbol of rebirth in Egyptian mythology and believed the dream might portend some sort of psychological rebirth that would pull her out of the excessive rationalism that had impeded her treatment. As he was about to say as much, he heard a tapping noise behind him and glanced around to see an insect fluttering at the glass. He opened the window, caught it, and discovered it was a beetle, the closest type his area had to a scarab beetle. Jung shared his interpretation of the dream, and from that moment forward the stunned patient started to improve.

Jung was just as startled as his patient by what had happened. Over the years, he continued to investigate the phenomenon, and coined the term *synchronicity* to describe such meaningful coincidences.

When we started our blog and invited other people to share their stories, we quickly discovered some people held misconceptions about what, exactly, a synchronicity is. Because examples often define something far better than a dictionary, let's start with a simple story.

While we were staying at a house in the Florida Keys, two friends came to visit—Robert from Stuart, Florida, and Robert from Minneapolis. For a couple of days, there were three Roberts at the house. One morning, one of the Robs was searching in the refrigerator for some jelly. He pulled out a jar of mango preserves called Robert Is Here. "Hey, you aren't going to believe this," he called out, laughing. "The jelly is onto us."

This synchronicity wouldn't have been nearly as interesting if just one Robert had been at the house. But three Roberts and finding the jam with that unusual name was enough to surprise even the skeptical Robert, whom we call Rabbit just to keep everyone straight. It actually awakened Rabbit to the idea of synchronicity. A few days later, he experienced a synchronicity of his own.

While we were staying on the island, Rabbit rode a bike that we had found in a storage room at the house. The bike had a sticker on it that read: Island Bikes, 900 Truman, Key West. He made several references to the bike shop, suggesting we should go there. One evening on the way to Key West for dinner, we happened to cross Truman at the 900 block, but were surprised to see a bike shop with a different name. It was closed, so we continued on. That seemed to be the end of it.

After we returned home, Rabbit stayed on in the Keys with another friend. During his stay, he was visited by a third friend, Toni, who came bearing a gift: a T-shirt from Island Bikes.

On the back of the shirt, below the name of the shop, was the new address. Mystery solved. Of course, Toni had no idea we'd discussed that very bike shop several times in recent days, or that Rabbit had been riding a bike purchased there. To top it off, the T-shirt featured bold green, red, and yellow stripes, the colors of the Rastafarian movement of Jamaica, Rabbit's usual winter destination.

Two days later, Rabbit burst through the door of our place, wearing his new T-shirt. "Hey, I had a synchronicity," he announced. "But what's it mean?"

In Jung's definition of the word, Rabbit had experienced the coming together of inner and outer events in a way that can't be explained by cause and effect and is meaningful to the observer. It certainly seized his attention and made him wonder if coincidences might be more than random events. After spending three days listening to us talk about synchronicities, he was primed to experience one. That's the beauty of the phenomenon. Once you become aware of synchronicities, they tend to proliferate. And as they increase in frequency, you can't simply keep ignoring them. You begin to dig for answers, to make associations, as Jung did between the golden scarab, rebirth, and his patient.

Sometimes, a single, dramatic experience is all it takes to awaken you to the magic that constantly hums around us, to how synchronicity is constantly at work in our lives. In the Minneapolis–St. Paul area, some urban explorers spend their free time exploring caves, mines, tunnels, rooftops, and basements. One of them, Gabriel Carlson, has a website where he writes about his passion: exploring these "spaces between, spaces forgotten, spaces forbidden."

In mid-January 2006, Gabe had a life-altering experience. He and a friend hiked to the end of Tomales Point in

California, the northernmost tip of land on the western side of the San Andreas fault line.

"We were surrounded on three sides by ocean, miles from the nearest road, buffeted by the wind cresting over the cliffs, in the most surreal, stunning landscape I have ever witnessed. The interplay of earth, water, light, and life were breathtaking, and the immediacy of the place and moment dwarfed all the things I'd thought were important to me back in civilization. I was washed away in experiencing the 'oneness' of all things."

In the aftermath of the experience, his intuition seemed sharper and an inner voice pulled him where he needed to go. After he returned from California, he and some friends went to a local thrift store "trolling for cool junk." Gabe was immediately drawn to an old teapot, but couldn't justify why he felt so compelled to buy it. He rarely wandered through the house wares section in the store and had never considered himself to be the type of person who would own—or buy—a teapot. "Finally, I decided to go along with my fading post—Tomales Point intuition kick and just let myself be guided—by instinct, by magic, by whatever the hell it is."

The teapot went home with Gabe, even though he couldn't figure out why it had seized his attention. He brewed some teabags in it. The tea was okay, but nothing special. "Over the next few days, I was disappointed when nothing really came of the purchase."

Within a week of buying the teapot, Gabe decided to explore the crawlspace in his house in Minneapolis, a place built in 1912. During his eight years of living in the house, he'd never felt the urge to venture into the crawlspace, an oddity for a guy who spends his free time exploring underground places.

The crawlspace had an access hatch in the wall, on the way to the basement. He found stuff: two dead mice, plastic sheeting, an old coffee can, rotting shoes. "As I crawled beneath the stairs, I felt something hard in the soft dirt beneath the plastic—a kind of domed bulge, sticking up slightly above the ground level." He pulled the object free, carried it out, and brushed off a corroded teapot. That's when he realized the significance of his discovery. "The teapot I'd just found buried under my house was identical to the teapot I'd brought home from the thrift store a few days earlier. Same design. Same size. Same materials. Same hinges. Same spout. The same teapot."

Gabe was a left-brain sort of guy, rational, skeptical, an atheist not given to mysticism. Yet, he followed his impulses and experienced a synchronicity so powerful that it changed him at a profound level. In an e-mail, which included a photo of the two remarkably similar teapots, he added, "I have become a regular experiencer and appreciator of synchronicity . . . and changed my beliefs about many things in the world. It's a far weirder and more wonderful place than I'd ever dared believe." Shortly after we posted his story, Gabe began his own synchronicity blog and continues to investigate the nature of the phenomenon.

Deciphering the Message

Deciphering the message is often the trickiest part of any synchronistic experience. What is the universe trying to tell you? Are you being warned? Is the experience a confirmation about something that's going on in your life? Is it a suggestion to turn in a different direction? Why did you attract this particular experience? What's the deeper meaning?

Let's say you've been experiencing clusters of numbers, 8s, for instance. What does 8 mean to you? What's the esoteric meaning of that number? Is it your lucky number? Blayne, a native of Wisconsin, had an interest in moving to Hawaii. He thought about it nearly every day and read everything he could find about the distant state. He also kept seeing 808 wherever he went—on license plates, in magazines and books. He didn't know what it meant until he stumbled on the answer—808 is the area code for Hawaii. It was as if the universe was subtly connecting him with his dream, and encouraging him to reach for it.

In the first part of this book, you'll not only learn the seven secrets of synchronicity, but discover how to decode your own synchronicities to enrich your life. In Part II, you'll learn how to engage synchronicity and to create fertile environments in which synchronicities can occur.

On your journey, you'll discover that synchronicities come in many guises. They can be as simple as thinking a word and then hearing that very word the moment you turn on the radio or TV. Or they can be as layered and complex as Gabe's teapot synchronicity. Sometimes a synchronicity seems to poke fun at you; other times it's as emotionally charged as a great novel. Synchronicities often address huge, sweeping themes that are common to all of us, what Carl Jung called archetypes.

The Collective Unconscious and Archetypes

In addition to the word synchronicity, Jung coined two other terms that are now well known: the *collective unconscious* and *archetypes*. As Deirdre Bair pointed out in her biography of

Jung, he arrived at his theories because he wasn't a typical psychoanalyst. Jung never went through formal analysis himself, "but used instead his 'personal myth' as the starting point to formulate what he believed were enduring objective truths. He juxtaposed his personal myth against the myths of many disparate cultures, eventually adding new terms to the common vocabulary and new ways of thinking about ideas."

The collective unconscious is like the DNA of the human race, a psychic repository of our history as a species. It contains images Jung called archetypes that are common to all people regardless of cultural background, nationality, or religious beliefs. We find these images in mythology, folklore, fairy tales, legends, hallucinations, fantasies, and dreams: mother, father, child, family, wise old man or woman, animal, hero, trickster, shadow, persona. And those are just the more universal images.

Archetypes represent our common experiences as human beings. When used effectively in movies and novels, they stay with us. One of the best-known examples of the trickster is Bugs Bunny. His trademark smirk and ever-present carrot are known around the world. The trickster is beautifully illustrated in the wizard from *The Wizard of Oz*. He portrayed himself as all-powerful, but his power was just smoke and mirrors, a trick of the light. He's also the embodiment of persona—our public faces, the masks we wear to create impressions on others.

Another vivid archetype is Darth Vader in the *Star Wars* movies. He actually embodies two archetypes: father and the shadow, that instinctive primal part of us where evil may reside. Hannibal Lecter from *Silence of the Lambs* depicts the shadow in its most perverse and evil form.

With synchronicities, we experience archetypes in different ways, sometimes as figures, but also as patterns of behavior, experiences, and situations. The quest is an archetypal situation in which the hero embarks on a journey to accomplish something—save the maiden, conquer the enemy, reclaim the kingdom. In *Star Wars*, Luke Skywalker's quest is to save Princess Leia and, ultimately, to defend the universe against Darth Vader. Your own personal quest might involve gaining admission to the college of your choice, finding your life partner, selling a novel or screenplay, or curing yourself of a disease.

Synchronicities often involve archetypes or archetypal situations, such as being picked on by the schoolyard bully in elementary school, loss of childhood innocence, the birth of a child, a wedding or divorce, the death of a parent. These types of events can foster synchronicities that startle us so deeply we are forced to recognize them as something more than random coincidences.

Mythologist Joseph Campbell experienced a startling synchronicity reminiscent of Jung's scarab while he was reading about the praying mantis, a hero symbol in the Bushman mythology. He was at home on the fourteenth floor of a building in Manhattan and had an urge to open a window, which he rarely did. A praying mantis stood on the rim of his window. Campbell, whose career focused on Jung's collective unconscious and mythology, said the mantis was huge and peered right at him. "Its face looked like the face of a Bushman. It gave me the creeps!"

What Are the Odds?

Odds are frequently an important component of synchronicity. Think of the last time you experienced something and were overwhelmed at the odds of that particular thing happening. As in Gabe's teapot story, the odds staggered your imagination.

It's the sort of story you tell at dinner parties. It awakened you to something. Perhaps it launched your search into the deeper meaning of life.

Improbable odds seize our attention, as in the three Roberts example we talked about earlier. What were the chances of our finding a jar of mango preserves called Robert Is Here? As if that wasn't strange enough, the very same afternoon Trish and two of the Roberts were at lunch in Key West, sitting at a courtyard table in Pepe's, when an elderly man came in with a beautiful golden retriever and took a seat in the waiting area. Because we used to have a golden, we always take note of them. Trish went over and asked the owner if she could pet the dog.

"You bet. He's friendly," the man said.

"We had to put down our retriever in May," Trish told him.

The man's face skewed with sympathy. He leaned toward the dog and spoke softly. "It's okay, Robert, she's a friend."

"Robert? His name is Robert?" The magic of the moment propelled Trish back to the table. "You aren't going to believe the retriever's name."

When Trish told the Robert story at a writers' conference, complete with the Rabbit nickname, a woman waved her arm in the air and apologized for interrupting. "But I just had to tell you that in my novel I have a character named Robert Rabbit."

When Anthony Hopkins was researching his part for the film of George Feifer's *The Girl from Petrovka*, he searched London bookshops for a copy of the novel. Unable to find one, he went into Leicester Square subway station to catch a train home. Lying on a bench in the station was the book, evidently left behind by a fellow traveler.

That in itself is astounding, but two years later, while in the midst of filming in Vienna, Hopkins was greeted on the set by

Feifer. The author mentioned that he no longer had a copy of his own book, and told Hopkins how he had lent his last copy to a friend who had mislaid it somewhere in London. Feifer added that it had especially annoyed him because he had annotated that particular copy. Scarcely believing such a coincidence could be possible, Hopkins handed Feifer the copy he'd found at the subway station. "Is this the one?" he asked. "With the notes scribbled in the margins?" It was indeed the book Feifer's friend had lost.

Taking Stock

Think of a meaningful coincidence, a sign, or an omen you experienced. What was going on in your life at the time? Were huge odds involved? Was it something you talked about with family and friends? Who else was involved? Anthony Hopkins's experience with the book he was looking for involved big odds and coincided with the movie project he was working on at the time. Did your meaningful coincidence, sign, or omen strike you as confirmation? A warning? Did it seem to be urging you to move in a new direction?

After writer Deirdre Bair had won the National Book Award for *Samuel Beckett: A Biography*, synchronicity played a role in the choice of her next project. "Suddenly, quite a lot of people who didn't know each other, and in several cases didn't know me, either, were asking what my next book might be and had I thought of writing about Jung?"

In the author's note at the beginning of *Jung: A Biography*, Bair writes that she was uncomfortable with the way Jung's name kept surfacing, but recognized the peculiar confluence of suggestions as a synchronicity. She began researching Jung's life and work. It felt right and the irony of the synchronicity was that she would be writing about the man who coined the term "synchronicity" and wrote extensively about it.

These kinds of synchronicities hint at a deeper order in the universe that physicist David Bohm called the implicate or enfolded order, a kind of primal soup that births everything in the universe. Bohm believes even time unfolds from the implicate order. He referred to our external reality as the explicate order. Synchronicity, then, is where the implicate and the explicate, the inner and the outer, coincide.

Lost and Found

When you lose something important, you usually become extremely focused. Whatever it is—your car key, your wallet, or your cell phone—you want it back. This single-minded determination and focus seem to initiate synchronicity, allowing you to recover what you lost, sometimes through extraordinary and unlikely means.

Tim Wallender, who lives in Memphis, Tennessee, related one of the most incredible instances of objects lost and found, which happened when he and his brother worked for the same railroad. His brother was an engineer at the time; Tim was a conductor. On the day the incident occurred, they were working on different trains.

"It was the first day that the railroad issued cell phones to the engineers. The engineer I was working with asked me who I thought would be the first one to lose their phone. I said without a doubt my brother would."

A few miles further down the track they had to stop and release some cars. Tim says this was about 120 miles from where both brothers started their trips, and only Tim's train was scheduled to stop there. "I set out the cars and engine and as I looked down in the snow there was a cell phone. My engineer was there to help with the hoses and we both looked at each other and said, 'No way.' Sure enough I open up the case and there was a sticker with my brother's name on it."

Tim called his brother that evening at the hotel where he was staying in Chicago and asked him where his phone was. He said he'd looked everywhere, but couldn't find it. "It turns out his second engine was giving him trouble and the cell phone must have fallen out of his pocket when he walked back to check it out. I don't know what the odds are of finding your brother's cell phone 120 miles from where he got it, the same day he got it, and only minutes after telling someone that he would lose it. Or what are the odds of stopping on top of it and looking down in the snow and finding it?"

Such stories seem to support the contention that we live in a giant hologram, where all information—past and future—is available to us. In an interview in *Psychology Today*, physicist Karl Pribram said, "if you . . . look at the universe with a holographic system, you arrive at a different view, a different reality. And that other reality can explain things that have hitherto remained inexplicable scientifically: paranormal phenomena, synchronicities, the apparent meaningful coincidence of events."

Synchronicity as a Wake-up Call

In the novel *Flatland: A Romance of Many Dimensions*, by Edwin Abbott, the conscious beings live in a two-dimensional world. A humble square, who narrates the story, dreams that he attempts to persuade the king of a one-dimensional world,

Lineland, that there is a second dimension. But the ignorant monarch won't listen. Later, the square is baffled when he encounters a sphere, who is on a mission to introduce the population of Flatland to depth. Finally, the square starts to comprehend the third dimension when he visits Spaceland.

In the same vein, you could think of synchronicity as a phenomenon introduced from a higher dimension that provides a glimpse into a reality that exists beyond our everyday notion of cause and effect.

A similar theme is presented in the movie *Pleasantville*. Brother and sister teens, David and Jennifer, played by Tobey Maguire and Reese Witherspoon, are catapulted into the black-and-white world of a 1950s sitcom, in which conformity is the ideal. But when Mary Sue, Jennifer's sitcom character, begins to question the reality of Pleasantville by asking her geography teacher what exists outside of the town, the insular world starts to break down: eventually color seeps into the world.

Again, the comparison can be drawn to synchronicity. When we become aware of coincidental events and recognize them as meaningful, they happen more frequently and "color" bleeds into our formerly black-and-white world.

Sometimes a synchronicity is a wake-up call, a way of reminding us that higher awareness is at play. When we're in the flow, we experience more synchronous events, more pleasure and less pain. Recognizing and following the flow of coincidences is our path to higher ground. When the synchronicities are dramatic, belief systems are radically changed, lives are profoundly altered. And occasionally, lives are saved and skeptics are turned into believers.

Jim, a mechanical engineer from Minneapolis, is a left-brain, scientific type who doesn't believe in mystical realms. In his free time, he explores caves, underground mines, and other hidden places, and is part of the same loosely formed group of urban explorers to which Gabe Carlson belongs.

Jim's frightening dream occurred on the morning he and some friends left on a road trip to Memphis to explore a large abandoned building. "In the dream, I was sitting in the middle of the woods. I'm not sure why I was there. Right next to me was a pile of dead branches. After a while, several snakes came out of the underbrush without warning and slithered around me really fast. They were about three feet long and were so close to me I thought they could kill me with one bite. I jolted awake."

He was startled and puzzled, but shrugged off the dream, and left that morning with his friend, Mario. Their first destination was a rural wooded area at the southern tip of Illinois, which has many underground silica mines. After exploring two mines in this area, they headed back to the car at a brisk pace, eager to catch up with the rest of their friends in Memphis. Jim wasn't paying attention to where he stepped until he heard a rustling sound in front of him. "I was moving so fast I didn't notice the enormous rattlesnake coiled up in the middle of the ridge until I was no more than five feet from it."

Jim's mind froze. He didn't have any idea how deadly the snake might be, but figured it was possible the poison would kill him before he could get help. He carefully backtracked a step or two, turned, and darted away.

"What are the odds of bolting awake from a dream about snakes and no more than six hours later finding myself a few feet from a rattlesnake in real life? Unbelievable. Part of my brain refuses to believe it really happened. One remarkable occurrence of synchronicity isn't quite enough to make me believe . . . but it does get me thinking about it." The dream snake was clearly Jim's wake-up call.

DEVELOPING AWARENESS

The best way to develop awareness of synchronicities—and, therefore, to experience more of them—is to keep track of them in a journal or in a computer file. Whenever you experience a seemingly coincidental event, take it seriously. Describe it in as much detail as possible.

- Note the time, date, and place where the synchronicity occurred.
- If another person or a group of people was involved, include their names and what they experienced. Did they recognize the synchronicity?
- Describe how you felt at the time it was happening.
- Try to link it to events taking place in your life.
- What symbols were involved?

Next, consider how the synchronicity might be meaningful.

- Does it affirm something you're feeling, doing, or contemplating?
- Does it transmit a message?
- Does it awaken you to a new path?
- Does it offer glimpses into the underlying order and beliefs in your life?
- Does it offer a tip about a certain pattern in your behavior?
- Watch for other related synchronicities that involve the same subject.

Over time, you may discover that many of your synchronicities are centered around particular themes—emotional highs and lows, creativity, your career, travel, family or friends, animals and pets. Once you recognize how and when synchronicities are most likely to occur for you, it's easier to attract them. When a synchronicity is repeated, or expanded upon, as in the Three Roberts story, your awareness of the outlandish odds increases and your ability to accept synchronicity expands.

Intuition is like a muscle. The more you use it, the stronger it becomes. The stronger it is, the greater the likelihood that you'll experience synchronicity more frequently and learn to use it as a compass to navigate your way through life.

In your journal, state a question. Keep it simple and specific. Instead of asking "Where is this relationship going?" ask "What is the true nature of this relationship?" Or, instead of asking if you'll get the new job, ask if it's the right job for you. Think about your question periodically as you read these chapters. By the end of the book, you'll have an answer, by using your intuition.

My Question:

will i visit Rachel in Australia

What is the best way for me to obtain money in order to be able to afford to buy land for ets.

Secret 2

THE HEART

The second secret reveals that synchronicities are deeply intertwined with our emotions.

"What if we valued feeling as much as thinking, as synchronistic events invite us to do?"

—ROBERT H. HOPCKE, *THERE ARE NO ACCIDENTS*

In a society that places the highest value on the objective mind, on the left brain's reasoning and rationale, emotions are often viewed with suspicion, as a pollutant of some kind. And yet, the very nature of a synchronicity is subjective and emotional. Synchronicity urges us to delve into the parts of ourselves that we may not be ready or willing to explore. Sometimes, synchronicities begin with an impulse to do something we've never done before. Such was the case for author Kurt Vonnegut.

One morning long before the days of the Internet and cell phones, Vonnegut felt compelled to call his brother-in-law, whom he'd never phoned before and had no reason to call. "I suddenly left my study . . . walked the length of the house to the phone in the kitchen, put in a long distance call to my brother-in-law." He had no idea that the man had died moments earlier.

As the phone rang, Vonnegut heard a breaking news report on the radio about a train that had plunged off an open draw-bridge in New Jersey. Even though his brother-in-law never took the train, Vonnegut instantly knew he was one of the passengers. Within an hour, the author was en route to New Jersey, where his sister was hospitalized with terminal cancer and her four children were now fatherless.

Before the sun set, Vonnegut had taken charge of the household and the kids. His sister died the next day. "My wife and I have since adopted and raised their children." Several weeks prior to the incident, Vonnegut's wife kept coming up with an odd notion: "The refugees are coming, the refugees are coming."

The Great Karass

Vonnegut's account of this dramatic event was included in author Alan Vaughan's *Patterns of Prophecies*. Vaughan

initially contacted Vonnegut to ask where he had come up
with the concept of the Karass in his novel *Cat's Cradle*. If
you've missed Vonnegut's brilliant novel, a Karass is a group
of people who are working together unknowingly as part of
a greater cosmic plan. You learn that you're part of a Karass
when meaningful coincidences occur between you and other
members of the Karass. However, in the cosmology of *Cat's
Cradle*, you must distinguish between chance coincidences
and meaningful ones. If you don't, you could be linked to a
Granfaloon, a false Karass.

Vonnegut's impulse to call his brother-in-law was strong
enough so that he acknowledged it as meaningful and acted on
it. He apparently knew it was not a Granfaloon.

We experience synchronicities for reasons that may not
be immediately obvious, and when they manifest themselves
through impulses, as in Vonnegut's case, we need to act, to
follow the impulse. Yes, our left brains will holler and shriek
about our irrational behavior and will hurl out numerous
reasons why the impulses should be ignored. But when we're
attuned to the reality of synchronicity and view coincidence as
meaningful, we become active participants in a deeper layer of
life. If we ignore the impulses, we do so at our own peril.

As F. David Peat noted in *Pathways of Chance*, "Synchronicities can occur when people enter into times of crisis or change,
when they are in love, engaged in highly creative work, or on
the verge of a breakdown. These are moments when the boundaries of mind and matter are transcended and people escape
from the normal hard and fast distinctions they make between
inner/outer, subjective/objective, psyche/matter."

It shouldn't come as any surprise, then, that during these
peak emotional experiences, synchronicities crash into our
lives. It's as if the universe is eager to offer guidance, to help us

move in the right direction, or to warn us that something big is around the bend and we should prepare for it now. In Vonnegut's terminology, we are all part of a great Karass.

Drama

Love can move mountains. This adage addresses the powerful, dynamic force of our emotions and the effect of this force on the physical world. When our emotions are heightened and our intentions are focused, stuff happens. The circumstances that trigger these emotions can range from dramatic life-changing transitions—birth, death, marriage or divorce, a move, heightened creativity—to the ordinary dramas we encounter in the course of our daily lives.

Here are some possible scenarios you might have experienced. Notice how each one is connected with a synchronistic event, something you might've ignored or barely noticed at the time.

1. You receive a reprimand or negative evaluation at work that you don't deserve. Shortly thereafter, you hear about a new job opening that fits your skills and expertise. You realize it's time to leave your present job.
2. At the moment a loved one dies, the clock stops. After the person's death, you often look at a clock at that exact time. You might see it as a curiosity, or as a message that we remain connected to loved ones even beyond this life.
3. During a heated argument, lights flicker, the power goes off, a transformer blows. The juxtaposition of events startles you into a deeper awareness of the dynamics of the relationship between you and the other person.

4. Your roommate moves out for no reason. Rather than blaming her or yourself, you try to maintain a friendship. While the two of you are traveling, you see a license plate on a car with your initials and the word *good,* a confirmation that you are doing the right thing.
5. You have a vision or dream of a person you're sure you've never met. Not long afterward, you meet that individual.

Think of an emotional time in your own life when your inner world seemed to coincide with an outer event. Did you dismiss the experience as random and without meaning? Or did you recognize the experience as significant? Were you able to use the synchronicity to make a decision?

Signs and Symbols

The great Karass of synchronicity speaks to us in many ways—through impulses, as in the Vonnegut example, and through emotions, relationships, dreams, visions, hunches, and symbols.

The words symbol and sign are often used interchangeably. Even in dictionaries, one is sometimes used to define the other. But the two words are actually quite different. A *sign* is any object, action, event, or pattern that conveys meaning and points to something definite, tangible, finite, knowable. When you approach an intersection and see a red sign shaped as an octagon, you step on the brakes. A *symbol* is an object, image, situation, or event that represents something else. Its full meaning may be blatantly obvious, or it may elude us or lie altogether beyond our comprehension.

"We are each surrounded by a vast landscape of symbols, encoded within the events and phenomena of our daily lives," writes Ray Grasse in *The Waking Dream: Unlocking the Symbolic Language of Our Lives*. A symbol might appear to you as a peculiar cloud pattern, the unexpected sighting of an animal, the discovery of an unusual object, a hidden message delivered in a casual conversation. Grasse calls these "environment symbols." They hold messages and clues about the patterns in our lives. The challenge lies in recognizing and interpreting these symbols. By becoming aware of them and understanding their significance, we gradually learn the language of symbols and are able to unlock the messages of such synchronicities more easily.

Robert Hopcke, in *There Are No Accidents*, relates a dramatic incident that occurred with a man whom he counseled during his days as an intern. The client had been dominated by his mother most of his life and believed that everyone around him—including Hopcke—only wanted to control and dominate him, just as she had done. They had reached an impasse in his therapy.

One rainy Sunday morning, Hopcke showed up for their regularly scheduled appointment and shortly before the start of their session, the power went out. His office admitted enough light, so they went ahead with their session. Things progressed as usual—going nowhere—and Hopcke decided to try a different approach. He pointed out that he'd shown up in a storm and conducted the session without any electricity in the building. Would he put up with such an unpleasant inconvenience if he was unconcerned about his client's welfare?

As Hopcke continued in this same vein, the client grew quiet and thoughtful, then said, "I see your point. Maybe you do care, maybe it isn't all about power."

Instantly, the power came back on, illuminating the office. Hopcke explained that the power outage and beginning the session in the darkness "reflected the emotional state of the relationship in which neither of us was able to see our way through to the light of awareness." But once he connected emotionally with his client, once the client got it and felt empowered again, "the office suddenly lit up with literal and emotional electricity."

Hopcke wrote, "In all synchronicities what is important is not the 'objective facts' of the coincidences but the emotional impact they had on the people involved . . . ."

Emotional impact: That's what moves mountains. And when we bring our intentions and desires into the equation, magic happens. There are times when we want something so badly and are willing to do the work necessary to bring about change that the universe responds quickly, literally, in a way we can't dismiss as random coincidence.

When our daughter Megan returned to college for her junior year, she felt somewhat unsettled because of a relationship that had ended the previous May. On the day she moved back into the dorm, the young man in question welcomed her with a big hug, but later in the day when they were hanging out with mutual friends, things between them were uneasy.

She's a proponent of the law of attraction—specifically through Esther and Jerry Hicks and the Abraham material—so she realized the importance of moving into a "better feeling place." She was looking for confirmation that she could do this.

That evening, she walked to Sarasota Bay to watch the sun set. Her cell phone was in her pocket, the keyboard unlocked. Anyone who has a cell knows that when the keyboard is unlocked and the phone is in your pocket, your body's movements can cause the phone to call random numbers, to type random text messages. The usual result is gibberish. But while Megan was sitting on the seawall, in a "perfect moment" of optimism, she felt her phone vibrating in her pocket.

"I slip it out, expecting to see the number of an incoming call," Megan recalls. "Instead, there's a text message that says BELIEVED 88. I didn't type this message. No one sent it to me. The message was created by my body's movements because the keypad wasn't locked. Even the word BELIEVED was spelled right! And 8 is my favorite number and this was double 8s. You guys call this synchronicity. To me, it means I was coming into alignment with Source. It was an affirmation."

The number 8 is the symbol for infinity. If the quantum physicists are right, if our intentions can affect matter, then Megan's experience seems to suggest that sometimes that effect can be stunningly literal. While consciously reaching for a better feeling, this message confirmed she was on the right path, she could move beyond the uneasiness.

Highs and Lows

If we are to benefit from a synchronicity, we must first recognize it as meaningful, then follow the clues and see where they lead. But when we're in the midst of crisis, following clues may not be as simple as putting one foot in front of the other. Sometimes, certain events need to take place before we can pursue the clues.

Such was the case for writer Sharlie West, whose husband died in 1989. A year later, her mother had a stroke and Sharlie had to admit her to a nursing home because she could no longer care for her. The facility was close by, though, and Sharlie visited her mother frequently. One afternoon during a visit, she and her mother were talking when, out of the blue, Sharlie said, "I should have married Jimmy B. He always cared about me."

Her mother looked at her, puzzled because Sharlie hadn't mentioned Jim's name in forty years. Then her mother remembered him. "He was head over heels for you," she remarked. They laughed about it. Sharlie forgot about the conversation, and three weeks later her mother passed away.

A few days later, Sharlie was sitting in the living room with a friend when suddenly she got the feeling that someone was thinking of her. "It was so intense I could feel the person in my mind and even see his image—middle-aged, salt-and-pepper hair, glasses. No one I knew. I mentioned it to my friend, who shrugged and said it was my imagination."

Then Sharlie received a letter of condolence from Jimmy B. He had read her mother's obituary in the paper and gotten her address from the funeral home. Sharlie was surprised, but recalled her conversation with her mother and marveled at the interesting timing of the events. Would Jimmy have attempted to contact her if he hadn't read her mother's obituary?

When Jimmy dropped by her house not long afterward, Sharlie was stunned. He was the same man she'd seen in her vision. Yet, the Jimmy she recalled was thin with dark hair and no glasses, so it would have been impossible for her to imagine him in the present. "Three weeks later, he moved in with me and eighteen years later, we're still together. We like to think my mom helped out."

What's particularly captivating about Sharlie's story is that her synchronicity involves three major emotional transitions over a period of about a year: the death of her husband, the death of her mother, and an encounter with the person she would marry. "In chance events both emotionally and symbolically meaningful, our psychological experience of a synchronicity always occurs to enable us to move forward in some way," writes Hopcke. "During such periods, the psyche sometimes provides, in the form of meaningful coincidences, a form of internal and psychological help."

FREUD, JUNG, AND THE CRACKING SOUND

Carl Jung experienced a powerful emotional synchronicity during a meeting with Freud in Vienna in 1909. At the time, the two men were still friends, but an undercurrent of tension existed in the relationship, probably due to what Jung later described as essential differences in their fundamental assumptions about the human psyche. When Jung asked Freud about his views on parapsychology, Freud sharply dismissed the entire field as nonsense. It stung Jung, whose own research was taking him deeper into the world of parapsychology, myth, religion, and symbolism, and he held back a sharp retort.

Suddenly, Jung felt as if his diaphragm were burning up, and right then, a loud cracking noise in a nearby bookcase startled both men. Jung suggested it was an example of a "catalytic exteriorization phenomena." When Freud dismissed that conclusion as "sheer bosh," Jung predicted it would happen again. And it did.

Writing about this incident in his autobiography, *Memories, Dreams, Reflections*, Jung noted that he never again discussed this incident with Freud. The implication is that it marked an important turning point in their relationship; Jung recognized his path was diverging from Freud's.

"It's as if this internal restructuring produces external resonance or as if a burst of mental energy is propagated outward into the physical world," writes Peat in *Synchronicity: The Bridge Between Mind and Matter*. "The cracking sound from Jung's bookcase is a clear example of such an externalization."

Jung believed that synchronicities peak during periods when deep unconscious forces are activated. This certainly fit the juncture he had reached as his work began to diverge from Freud's theories. It was also true for Hopcke's client when he finally grasped that not everyone was out to control him.

If Not for Love, Then What?

The heading for this section is taken from a popular bumper sticker. It captures the essence of love as a force of nature, and serves to remind us that when we act from a place of love— rather than from bitterness, anger, resentment, or some other negative emotion—the synchronicities that often accompany tragedy can provide deeper insights and even reassurance.

In 1993, Debra Page, a California psychic, gave birth to her second daughter, Laryssa. The baby, born with a rare, spontaneous genetic mutation, was given twelve days to live. She beat the odds, however, and lived for nearly two years. During that time, Debra and her husband met many wonderful, helpful people from the local hospice who came to their home to help with Laryssa's care. The child died on October 9, 1995.

In 2007, Debra and her husband were trying to locate a physician to treat Debra's chronic autoimmune disorder. A neighbor, who worked in the administration of the largest hospital system in San Diego, put her in touch with a doctor who was supposedly the best in the area and who was taking new patients. The day of her appointment, Debra and her husband waited in the office for the doctor to come in. When she did, she read through Debra's medical history and started to cry. "I know you both. I worked with Laryssa as a volunteer."

Debra suddenly remembered her, too, a sweet young woman who had lost her mother to cancer. "We all cried and hugged. Then she said that she has a daughter now. I asked when she was born, and the doctor replied, 'October 9, 1995.' The very day Laryssa died. We were all amazed at the coincidences."

Debra was able to embrace this synchronicity as a "beautiful gift from the past." It was as if her daughter had reached out to help her find not only the physician she needed, but a woman who had cared for Laryssa herself during her final days and weeks of life, and whose daughter was born on the very day that Laryssa died.

Connections to People

Our relationships provide richly textured atmospheres for the occurrence of synchronicity. Friendships connect us to something larger than ourselves, awakening us to a mysterious realm that exists outside of cause and effect. You might make a new acquaintance and discover you and your friend have similar interests, have had similar experiences, and even know some of the same people. You might encounter friends in places where you wouldn't expect to know anyone.

Take a few minutes to think about the people outside of your own family who have played important roles in your life. Note how you met, and the reasons your friendship developed. Look for anything extraordinary or mysterious in the original encounter. For example, Rob met his friend Rabbit, mentioned in the first chapter, during college when they both arrived simultaneously on bicycles at a raging fire that destroyed a dance studio near the campus. They discovered they both lived on the same block and had friends in common.

Synchronicity often occurs when old friends are about to resurface in our lives. It can unfold through a word, a thought, an object, even through the name of a particular fish. Richard Arrowsmith of the Scottish Highlands went fishing one fall day with his father and two young daughters. Throughout the day, his daughters pulled in one mackerel after another, but Richard didn't even get a nibble. Finally, toward evening, they decided to pack up their things. The wind had picked up, the sky sagged with clouds. Richard didn't want to leave empty-handed, so he cast out once more, confident he would catch something.

Suddenly, he felt a sharp tug on the line and his rod bent to the point where he thought it might snap in two. He reeled in "a whopper." He didn't know what kind of fish it was, but his father informed him it was a pollock. Because they had tossed the mackerel back into the ocean, they decided to take the pollock home for dinner.

It was the first time Richard had eaten pollock. The fish was large enough to feed the entire family, the dog, and the cats. This single catch turned into a celebration.

Later that evening, Richard checked his e-mail and found one new message. It came from Iain Pollock, an old friend he hadn't seen or spoken to in more than three years.

"We used to be work colleagues but when I moved to another job we simply lost touch with one another. The e-mail from Iain Pollock came completely unannounced. The fact that he decided to resume contact on the very same evening I caught and ate my first ever pollock boggles my mind."

Where Do You Place Your Attention?

Anything in your environment can hint at synchronicity. In the course of a given day, notice where you place your attention. Is there a particular corner or neighborhood that you pass on the way to work that always seems to reach out to you? How does it make you feel? Why does it attract you? It may be that you're tuning in emotionally to a synchronicity that lies ahead. That's what happened to Adele Aldridge.

During a difficult period in her life, Adele was seeing a therapist in New York City and used to drive down West Side Highway to get to the therapist's office. On the drive, she always passed a giant cigarette billboard with a picture of a tall handsome man smoking a Winston.

"I found the image compelling and upsetting at the same time. I was drawn to look at it and at the same time, being a very insecure driver, knew it was dangerous for me to drive and look at that billboard." It happened every time she drove the route for the next eight months, an attraction and compulsion that baffled her.

Then one night in the dead of winter, with the wind howling outside her bedroom window, she came across the same advertisement in a magazine. The image evoked all sorts of feelings that made no sense to her. "I found the man hypnotically attractive, but also hated him. Suddenly I spat at the picture." It shocked her so deeply that she was sure she had gone off the deep end. She never told anyone about this—not even her therapist.

Nine years later, when Adele was living in California, she and a friend went to No Name Bar in Sausalito to listen to jazz. During a break, the good-looking drummer came over and sat at their table. Adele felt deeply attracted to him, but also troubled for no apparent reason. One thing led to another and they made a date to go into San Francisco the following week.

As soon as she got into his car, he pulled out a postcard of the image on that billboard on West Side Highway. It was the same man. She hadn't recognized him immediately because it was nine years later and he was fifty pounds heavier. When she saw the picture, she screamed—certainly not the response the drummer was expecting. She told him she had a love/hate relationship with that picture. His response? "I think you still have a love/hate relationship."

You get what you concentrate on: that's the basis of the law of attraction. Adele's emotional reaction to the man on the billboard was apparently so powerful that it reverberated through time, attracting the synchronous encounter with this very individual nine years later. Think about the odds. Adele had moved across the country, just happened to go to a particular bar in Sausalito on the very night this man was playing there, and he just happened to come over to her table. At any juncture in the nine years, a single different decision could have changed the circumstances.

The message to take from her experience is stunningly simple. If you have powerful negative emotions that you carry around with you, then the synchronicities you experience related to those emotions are likely to be negative. Isn't it preferable to move through life from a place of love rather than hatred, anger, or hostility?

BREATH WORK

As you work consciously with your emotions, pay close attention to your breathing. Awareness of your breath— how you inhale, exhale, how deep your breaths are, how slowly or rapidly you exhale—grounds you emotionally. Once you're aware of your breath, slow it down. Breathe more deeply. As your breath slows, you'll feel calmer, more relaxed. It will be easier to appreciate everything that's right in your life and to conjure happier emotions. If you don't already meditate, try it for five minutes a day for a month. You may notice an appreciable difference in your emotions—and an increase in the synchronicities you experience.

You may want to do what author, publisher, and medical intuitive Louise Hay does every morning. Before she even gets out of bed, she expresses her gratitude for everything in her life. It's a beautiful habit to cultivate. And the universe will always respond by bringing more experiences, situations, and people into your life to appreciate.

Connections to Places

At some time in your life you may feel strongly connected to a particular place. It might be a city or section of a country, a stretch of beach or a nook in a forest, a certain house or piece of land. These connections are intensely emotional, archetypal, and often psychic in that they speak to some deeper level.

Such an intense connection can be an invitation to experience another aspect of yourself. Perhaps it's a connection that seems to complete you in some way, or it makes a statement about who you really are or wish to become. It might be a vacation destination that you visit over and over. One day you realize it's not only your favorite destination, it's where you want to live. Then, you hear about a job opening that would require you to move to the town or city of your dreams.

Sometimes, this connection is so emotionally charged it draws a particular experience your way through the law of attraction and awakens you to some greater potential. That's what a certain house in Big Sur did for Darryl Armstrong, a chiropractor in Kentucky.

Several years ago, during the early days of establishing his business, Darryl visited a friend in Carmel, California.

He'd always wanted to tour the area, especially around Big Sur, so he spent time driving and exploring the Pacific Coast Highway.

By chance, he saw a large cabin that hung off the side of a cliff with a remarkable view of the Pacific Ocean. "It was obvious someone had spent a great deal of their personal time and money carving out this homestead. I was mesmerized. I could imagine what life might be like in a cabin by the sea."

Whenever he was on the West Coast, Darryl drove by that cabin. Over time, the property changed. A fence went up on the road, a gate was installed. But he could still see the cabin and it always fed his imagination. He wondered what it would be like to live there by the sea.

A few years after discovering the cabin, he was headed home to his own "cabin in the woods" on Lake Barkley in Kentucky. He took a late-night Southwest flight. Exhausted, Darryl settled into his preferred exit-row seat and stretched out. "I normally hibernate on a plane and rarely strike up conversations. The plane wasn't very full but, sure enough, this fellow chooses to sit in the exit row with me. For some reason I was drawn to his smile and immediately liked him. Eventually my southern hospitality overcame me, I guess, and since I had plenty of coupons, I offered him a drink and he smiled and offered me one as well."

As they chatted, Darryl discovered the man was from California. They started talking about how they both were drawn to certain areas. Darryl mentioned Monterrey, Carmel, Big Sur. When Daryl got to the story about the cabin overlooking the ocean, the man's expression changed. Daryl didn't think anything of it. He just continued describing the setting and how much he would love to live there, with the view and the peace and quiet.

The man finally replied that he understood how Darryl felt, that they both obviously worked hard so when they got home, they became hermits. Then he reached into his briefcase and pulled out a photo. "You guessed it. This was the man who owned the cabin I have always cherished in my mind. We were both surprised, yet it seemed as if a 'loop' had been closed. I left the plane that night knowing that someone with whom I shared a mutual empathy enjoyed the cabin by the sea as much as I did."

For Darryl, something fundamental changed in the way he perceived the world. The cabin and the dramatic scenery by the sea called out to him, he felt compelled to answer the call, and his desire attracted the meeting with the cabin's owner. Again, what are the odds these two men would meet on a random flight, sit across from each other, and strike up a conversation? Who's orchestrating this stuff, anyway?

Physicist F. David Peat was probably wondering that when a small town in Italy called out to him. "In 1994, some time after David Bohm had died, I agreed to write his biography. I visited relatives in the U.S., then decided I'd need to spend time in London," says Peat. Through an agency, he arranged to rent an apartment in London for several months, beginning on December 15, 1994. Peat and his wife put their house in Ottawa up for rent and soon received a generous purchase offer, with the condition that they had to be out by the beginning of August.

This time frame meant Peat and his wife had three months to kill before their apartment in London would be available. They considered finding another place in Ottawa, but Peat's wife, Maureen, loved the Sienese school of painting, so they asked an Italian travel agent to find them an apartment in Siena.

"For several days before we left, I kept asking the agent for an address and phone number to pass on to friends. Then on the day we left for the airport she admitted that the apartment had fallen through but she had gotten us a room. When we arrived, we realized the room wasn't in Siena itself but some distance outside—we had to take a bus. It was just a small bedroom normally used by students and lacked privacy."

They arrived on August 5 and started visiting various agencies in Siena, looking for a place to rent for the next few months. It was the month of the Palio—the big horserace in Siena—and the town was packed with tourists. The couple visited every agency on the list, but nothing was available.

By August 8, it was clear that they had nowhere to stay. They wondered if they should return to Canada or fly to Portugal, where they had friends. While waiting for a bus, Peat saw a plaque on a door in the square. It was an agency, but not one on the official list he had. He went inside and was told to return the next day.

On August 9, they took a bus into Siena again. His diary entry for that date reads: "Very nervous about going in as everything is staked on the last throw. So walked a bit first. Two Germans stopped in the road looking at a green-gold scarab."

The golden scarab held a special significance for Peat because it was the very creature that triggered Jung's investigation of synchronicity. Excited, he turned to Maureen. "Now we'll get something!"

He went into the building and, sure enough, the secretary told him a friend had a house for sale in the village of Pari, in Tuscany, and might be willing to rent. On August 27, they moved into the house in Pari and stayed until December 15. Their intention at that time was to live in London and leave Canada forever.

A year later, Peat was invited to a conference in Italy. It was a long haul from the airport, so he and Maureen decided to go via Pari and stayed at a local hotel that night. The next morning when they looked out the window, they saw someone they had known in Pari the previous year. The man told them about a house for rent in town. "At this time there were no 'foreigners' in Pari and it was rare to rent a house because all the houses were owned by families and had been passed down for generations. My wife saw the house and said we'd take it. In 1996 we became permanent residents. In many ways we feel that the village had called us, that this was the place where we were supposed to live."

Peat now runs the Pari Learning Center in Tuscany. Guest lecturers, artists, writers, and thinkers teach workshops and seminars there on new paradigms, creativity, and, of course, synchronicity.

PAY ATTENTION TO YOUR FEELINGS

Your emotions are an accurate barometer of what is right, wrong, or unsettled in your life. So whenever you experience a synchronicity, make note of your emotional state. Were you in an optimistic mood? Were you happy, feeling low, or somewhere in between? What or whom were you thinking about at the time?

When you feel out of sorts, list the thing in your life that you would most like to change. Maybe you would like a nicer place to live, a better job, a car that doesn't give you trouble. Remember, you can't change other people no matter how much you would like to do so. But you *can* change yourself.

Next, list the things you love about your life. Strive to elevate your mood by conjuring a happier thought, a fond memory, anything that makes you smile or laugh.

Now you're ready for the magic. Watch for a synchronicity that reminds you of what's right in your life. Once you elevate your mood, chances are a synchronicity will manifest that not only reflects your improved mood, but also offers guidance, insight, and hope, as BELIEVED 88 did for Megan. Keep in mind that the entire experience probably won't happen in the same hour, even the same day. The synchronicity might appear a week or two later. The point is that you'll recognize it and apply the meaning to your life. With any luck, it will address one of the items you wrote down on your list of things that you would like to change in your life.

Secret 3

THE THEORY

Synchronicity is the granddaddy of all paranormal phenomena, telepathy, precognition, clairvoyance, and remote viewing.

"The unseen design of things is more harmonious than the seen."

—HERACLITUS

For the moment, forget whatever you think you know about psychic phenomena. Forget *The X-Files*, *Medium*, *Ghost Whisperer*. Instead, recall the last time you had a hunch about something, a gut feeling, and acted on it. Or, think about the dream you had that later came true. Or, consider how you often know what your partner is going to say before he says it. If you've experienced something like this—and most of us have—then you're already familiar with psychic phenomena and with synchronicity, which lies at the heart of all things psychic.

We're All Connected

Carl Jung maintained that synchronicity is the basis for all psychic phenomena. Jung's own visions during a vivid near-death experience after a heart attack in 1944 influenced this belief. He soared high above the earth until he saw it as a blue globe, then swept across the deserts of Arabia, over the snow-covered Himalayas, and into a temple in India. He was certain he had died and was about to meet "all those people to whom I belong." Then, to his disappointment, he was pulled back to Europe, to the hospital, and into his body. He believed that experience was real, not imagined.

In his biography, *Memories, Dreams, and Reflections*, Jung wrote, "We shy away from the word 'eternal,' but I can describe the experience only as the ecstasy of a non-temporal state in which present, past and future are one. Everything that happens in time had been brought together into a concrete whole. Nothing was distributed over time, nothing could be measured by temporal concepts."

HOW ATTUNED ARE YOU?

In order to experience synchronicities more frequently, strive to be open and receptive to intuitive experiences. Check the statements in the list below that apply to you.

- Even in a crowded parking lot, are you usually able to "create" a space?
- If you need information in a hurry, does the information somehow instantly turn up?
- Are you able to recall your dreams in detail?
- Have you received answers or insights from your dreams?
- Do you believe there's more to the universe than what you see?
- When you're blocked from attaining something you desire, do you consider it an opportunity?
- When one door closes for you, does another open quickly?
- Have you had a premonition that later came true?
- Do you look for patterns in your own life—in behavior, relationships, jobs?
- Have you experienced telepathy?
- Do you sometimes know an e-mail from a particular person or about a particular event will be in your inbox even before you open it?
- Do you easily pick up on the moods of loved ones?
- When something traumatic happened to a loved one, did you sense it before you were told?
- When you meet someone for the first time, do you have an immediate sense about the individual?
- Have you ever needed a certain sum of money to cover an unexpected expense and that exact sum came to you?

- In a job interview, do you know before the interview is done whether you'll get the job?
- Have you ever held an object and picked up information from it that was later verified?
- At historic or ancient sites, do you feel emotions that aren't your own?
- Do you use any sort of divination system for insights and guidance?
- When a "coincidence" happens, do you look for the deeper meaning?

If you checked

15–20: You're open and receptive, and probably experience synchronicities frequently.

10–15: You probably experience synchronicities, but perhaps not as frequently as you would like.

0–10: Push open that inner door. A magical universe awaits you on the other side.

Psychic experiences emanate from what physicist David Bohm called the implicate order. In Bohm's view of the universe—and in Jung's—these aspects of synchronicity provide vital clues to how we're all connected. Physicist Victor Mansfield agrees. As he wrote in *Synchronicity, Science, and Soul-Making*, we live in "a radically interconnected and interdependent world, one so essentially connected at a deep level that the interconnections are more fundamental, more real than the independent existence of the parts."

These ideas are echoed in Eastern spiritual traditions that date back thousands of years. In the Indian sacred text, the *Rig Veda*,

Indra—the king of gods and god of war—casts a great spiritual net (known as Indra's Net) in which all members of the cosmos are interconnected. In *Synchronicity in Your Life*, Shawn Randall speculates that if the "net is multi-dimensional, the points where the strings of the net connect would be like intersecting points from which one could access the whole net. . . . Basically, this is how synchronicity works." In other words, one tug ripples across the entire net.

The *Bhagavad Gita*, the Hindu religious poem, recognizes the synchronous nature of creation and an underlying cosmic unity. The Hindu term, *Brahman*, refers to the fundamental connection of all things in the universe. The appearance of this universal oneness in the soul is called *Atman*.

Zen Buddhism refers to *satori*, a sense of unity felt with the universe and an awareness of the compassionate intelligence that permeates the most minute details. *Pratitya-samutpada*, a doctrine of Buddhist philosophy, especially in China and Korea, translates as "dependent arising" and refers to an interdependent web of cause and effect, the motivating principle of the universe.

Chi, according to Chinese philosophy, is the life force that permeates all things and empowers the universe. In yoga philosophy, chi is comparable to *pranayama*, and is manifested in humans through the breath.

These Eastern ideas are similar to the concept of the noosphere, a notion created by Pierre Teilhard de Chardin, a French philosopher, paleontologist, and ordained Jesuit priest. He was convinced of the existence of an invisible "ordering intelligence," a mental sphere that linked all humanity. He proposed that as mankind organizes itself in more complex social networks, the noosphere expands in awareness.

Premonitions and Precognition

Premonition is usually defined as a feeling of anticipation or anxiety about future events. Precognition is defined as knowledge of a future event or situation.

For instance, imagine you have a feeling that you should turn at a particular intersection, even though it's not on your usual route to work. You later discover there was a huge accident on your usual route that tied up traffic. That's a premonition. But if you dream someone hands you a phone message that reads *Your uncle has just passed away*, and he dies two weeks later, that's precognition—foreknowledge of future events that can occur moments or decades before the event unfolds.

Both intuitive abilities originate in the nonlocal mind, which operates outside the boundaries of normal space and time. "By its nature, nonlocal mind connects all things because it is all things," wrote Deepak Chopra in *The Spontaneous Fulfillment of Desire*.

When he was just a boy, Keith Fraser, a university records keeper in Aberdeen, Scotland, had a precognitive experience about the woman he eventually married. During visits to his grandmother's house in the early 1960s, Keith read copies of D. C. Thompson's *The Friendship Book* to pass the time. The book contained a number of photographs, and one of a young girl painting a picture captured his attention.

Years later, while visiting his girlfriend's home for the first time, he noticed a copy of *The Friendship Book* on a bookcase. He mentioned that he used to read it when he visited his grandparents, and started to flip through the book. "It was then that I saw a photograph I recognized—of a small girl painting a picture. I pointed this out to my future in-laws and imagine my surprise when they said the photo was of my future wife, which they had submitted to the publisher, D. C. Thompson, in the early 1960s."

When Ray Getzinger was twelve, he used to dream about a redheaded woman from Georgia who wore her hair in ringlets. Ten years later, in 1966, he married a woman with red hair who lived in Virginia but was born in Georgia. "Before we had been married a year she styled her hair exactly as I had dreamed."

Both Keith and Ray were obviously impressed enough by their early experiences to remember them, so that when the actual women appeared in their lives, they recognized the stunning synchronicities. Their stories exemplify how synchronicities connect us to something larger than ourselves, to what is essentially invisible and unknowable. But if, as quantum physicists and mystics say, the nonlocal mind exists outside the usual boundaries of space and time, then perhaps the child Keith and the dreaming Ray were dipping into future possibilities.

In her book, *Synchronicity: The Promise of Coincidence*, Deike Begg wrote, "The most interesting aspect of all truly synchronistic phenomena is that there appears to be a pre-existing knowledge of things to come, things of which we have at that moment no apparent awareness whatsoever. There seems to be an altogether 'other' that knows more than us, can see into the future and also has the ingenious ability to find the quickest route to return us to our destined path."

SENSING THE FUTURE

Like Keith and Ray, you can peek into the future. Here's how to do it.

As we explained in the previous chapter, emotions often play a role in synchronicities, including incidents of precognition. Think about an important relationship

outside of your immediate family, especially a love interest. Try to remember the first time you met. Did you feel
an immediate connection, sense that a close, long-term
relationship would develop? Were there any physical
sensations that triggered your thoughts? Some people
feel their teeth tingling or "growing" during important
encounters that will affect their futures. Others have
predictive dreams or receive flashes of images related to
future events.

You might think such things don't happen to you, but
maybe they do, and you never noticed. Pay close attention to your thoughts and feelings as important events
unfold in your life. Watch for patterns. Keep a journal. Try
to guess what will come about, based on your intuitive
thoughts and feelings. Later, look back and see how well
you did.

Also, keep track of your dreams, even if they don't seem
to make sense at the time. Use a notebook or journal, or
a file on your computer. You might be surprised later on to
realize that a dream seemed to preview your future. Before
going to bed, suggest to yourself that you'll have a dream
of an upcoming event.

Upon awakening, jot down any dream images you
remember. Don't try to interpret them, but note as many
details as possible. Pay attention to the people, the scenery, and the main incident.

Note how you felt during the dream. Were you energized
and joyful? Filled with fear and dread? Calm and observant? Or were you agitated? About once a month, review
your dreams to see if any of the scenarios actually hinted
at future events.

Most of your dreams will be symbolic messages con-
cerning things taking place in your life at the time. But
occasionally, especially if you're nudging your dream self
before falling asleep, you'll probably discover dreams that
foretell events in your life. When you do, note how you felt
during the dream. That might help you recognize other
precognitive dreams.

Peeking into the Future

It's also possible to consciously and intentionally peek into the
future—even the distant future. In the late 1980s, our friend
Renie Wiley offered to progress us hypnotically into the future.
Renie wasn't a professional hypnotist, but had practiced hyp-
nosis on family and friends. She also had a soothing voice and
an infallible relaxation technique. As she spoke, Trish suddenly
saw herself as a tall woman, completely bald, living in a domed
city.

"Why are the people living in domes?" Renie asked.

"It's safer in the dome," Trish replied. "Outside, the air is
bad, it's a wilderness."

"Do all people live in domes?"

"Only the lucky ones. We aren't many. There are a few other
domes."

"How old are you?"

"Late twenties."

"Why are you bald?"

"Genetic. We're all bald."

"What year is it?" Renie asked.

"I don't know."

Trish was deeply unsettled by this progression. It felt real. She could sense the texture and reality of this young woman's life.

Not long afterward, we ran across *Mass Dreams of the Future*, by Helen Wambach, PhD, and Chet Snow. Dr. Wambach, a past-life regressionist for nearly thirty years, discovered she could progress people into their future lives. She began a painstaking project in France and the United States where she progressed 2,500 people. She passed away before the project was completed, but Dr. Chet Snow finished the work and published the findings.

Most of the individuals who participated agreed that in the future the population of the earth was vastly diminished. The futures they experienced fell into four distinct categories: a sterile and joyless world, where most people lived in space stations and ate synthetic food; a world in which people lived in harmony with nature and with each other; a post-nuclear world populated by survivalists; and a future in which people lived in underground cities enclosed by domes. We were stunned by the parallels.

Snow explained the four different scenarios as probabilities only, potential futures that we're creating through our collective consciousness. He subsequently released a map of what the United States might look like after earth changes he believed would occur between 1998 and 2012. Yet, he recommends that people visualize a more positive future. As he wrote in *Mass Dreams*, "If we are continually shaping our future physical reality by today's collective thoughts and actions, then the time to wake up to the alternative we have created is now. The choices between the kind of Earth represented by each of the types are clear. Which do we want for our grandchildren? Which do we perhaps want to return to ourselves someday?"

Psychic Children

Psychic ability is common among children. Whether it's due to their lack of social conditioning or to something else, they can be gifted telepaths or clairvoyants. Perhaps the future is as accessible to them as the present. To help your child develop her psychic ability, try this game while you're in the car. The car's motion tends to be relaxing, inducing a kind of trance.

Set the stage. Tell your child you're going to play a game with colors. One of you will be the sender, who will think of a bright, vivid color. The other will be the receiver, who should say the first color that comes to mind. Then reverse your roles. Or you could ask your child what event she thinks might occur in his life tomorrow. Or next week. The results may astonish you.

These kinds of psychic games help a child's perceptions to develop in a different way. She learns to rely on her own instincts and intuition.

We played these games often with our daughter, Megan, when she was young. But we were surprised when, in third grade, she tuned in on an event that would impact our family.

During a Thanksgiving program in elementary school, Megan showed a dog she'd sculpted from clay and announced she was grateful for the golden retriever she was going to get. We were puzzled. We had no plans to get any kind of dog. After all, we had three cats. But shortly before Christmas, a family friend asked if we would adopt a golden retriever that needed a home. We agreed to keep the dog for a week to see how she got along with the cats. The retriever, Jessie, immediately got along famously with the cats, settled in front of Rob's desk, and found a new home.

Megan's desire for a dog was strong and pervasive, so she undoubtedly attracted the circumstances and opportunity for obtaining one. But how did she get the breed right? Not only was her sculpture a synchronicity, it was specifically precognitive.

Telepathy

Telepathy is unspoken communication—we pick up the thoughts, feelings, and sensations of others. Most of us have experienced it at one time or another, often with someone to whom we're close. You've probably heard someone say, "I was just about to say that." Or you're just about to pick up the phone when it rings and it's the person you intended to call.

Imagine you've just visited your elderly father who lives alone. You're almost home when you hear his voice in your mind calling for help. At first you dismiss it as a reflection of your concern about your father's health. But the voice in your head is persistent. You call your father on your cell and, when there's no answer, your concern grows. You turn around and drive back to his apartment. You find him on the floor, unable to get up and answer the phone.

Jung, in his autobiography, describes a telepathic experience with one of his patients. He had gone out to deliver a lecture, then returned to his hotel around midnight, but had trouble falling asleep. "At about two o'clock . . . I woke with a start, and had the feeling that someone had come into the room; I even had the impression that the door had been hastily opened. I instantly turned on the light, but there was nothing." Jung thought another guest must have opened his door by mistake, but when he looked out into the hallway, "it was as still as death."

He struggled to remember what had happened and recalled he had been awakened "by a feeling of dull pain, as though something had struck my forehead and then the back of my skull." The next day, Jung received a telegram informing him that his patient had committed suicide by shooting himself. "Later, I learned that the bullet had come to rest in the back wall of his skull."

Jung said he felt this experience was a genuine synchronistic phenomenon commonly associated with an archetypal situation—in this instance, death. He believed his knowledge of the patient's death had been made possible because in the collective unconscious, time and space are relative. "The collective unconscious is common to all; it is the foundation of what the ancients call the 'sympathy of all things'. . . the unconscious had knowledge of my patient's condition."

TELEPATHIC SENDING EXERCISE

Try this exercise in telepathic sending. Think of someone you want to call you. The other person isn't aware of your desire. Begin with someone who might easily decide to give you a call. Write down the target's name. Relax. Breathe deeply. Imagine a setting involving the person. If you know exactly where the person is and what her surroundings look like, visualize them.

Next, focus on the person. Picture her face and what she might be doing. Imagine her smiling as she decides to phone you. Imagine her dialing your number. You answer and she identifies herself and asks how you are. Focus on this scenario for a few minutes, then let go of the image.

If you don't get a call within a short period of time, phone the person. Ask her what she's doing and if she's been thinking about you. She might've considered calling you, but got too busy. If so, ask what time she began thinking of calling you. Does it correspond with when you sent her a message?

If you don't get a "hit," try the experiment with another person you know.

Clairvoyance

Have you ever wished you could be the proverbial fly on the wall? That you could visit a certain time or place and see what was happening, without anyone knowing you were there?

Wishful thinking? Not necessarily.

Clairvoyance, a French word that means "clear seeing," is a psychic skill that falls within the realm of synchronicity, as Jung described it. It's an extrasensory talent that allows you to see something beyond the range of your normal vision. In other words, you project a part of your mind elsewhere. Another popular term for the talent is remote viewing, which came into our lexicon when the U.S. military used psychic spies.

How is this possible? While your brain is a physical receptor, your mind exists beyond the limits of your body. You may not realize it, but you can send your mind to distant places to pick up information. In fact, you do it when you're sleeping. Research has shown that everyone, with practice, can attain some degree of clairvoyance. Sometimes it happens spontaneously. For example, in 1759, Emanuel

Swedenborg, a Swedish scientist, inventor, and mystic, told a group of guests that a great fire was raging in Sweden, 300 miles away. Later, his statement was confirmed. Because no telephones, radio, television, or Internet existed in Swedenborg's time, such an ability was a valuable skill.

REMOTE VIEWING EXERCISE

Even if you've never had a spontaneous clairvoyant experience, you can learn techniques to help you glimpse scenes taking place elsewhere. Although this book isn't intended as an instruction guide for learning psychic skills, here is an exercise that was developed at the Stanford Research Institute. It's a good one to use for your first attempt at remote viewing.

You'll need at least one friend, preferably two, to participate. One person goes into another room and chooses a small object, then places it in a bag, box, or envelope so that you can't possibly know what it is. The best objects are those with sensory details. A piece of sandpaper, for example, has color, texture, and sound attached to it. A tomato has scent, color, texture, and shape. Your friend must stay in the other room, so as not to give you any clues.

Your mission is to identify the object, using your psychic power. Close your eyes and begin to write or tape-record your impressions. If you prefer, draw the object.

If no impressions come to mind, try to look into the future and see the object being placed in your hand at the end of the exercise. Or, go into the past and see your friend slipping the object in the bag, box, or envelope. Use all your senses. Let yourself see, feel, smell, hear, and taste the object. Don't try to guess what it is;

allow your impressions and the sensory information to accumulate.

Meanwhile, a second friend (if available) asks questions that guide you to new ways of experiencing the object and keep you on track. For example, if you're describing a round, red object, your friend might ask you about its texture or smell. He might suggest that you observe the object from a different angle. However, it's important this second person doesn't know the object's identity. Otherwise, he could inadvertently drop clues.

Stop when you run out of impressions. Set a time limit of ten or fifteen minutes, then you're goign to reverse your roles. Ask the first friend to bring you the object he selected. Hold it in your hands. Feel it and sense all its qualities. Note which characteristics come through to you clearly and which ones are faint or missed altogether. Did you get sidetracked by the tendency to overanalyze? Learn to distinguish between the mind's idle chatter and psychic functioning. Remote viewing usually manifests as subtle, fleeting messages or images that come to mind when you quiet the chatter.

Advanced Remote Viewing

Of course, advanced remote viewers take on much more complex "targets." Even with modern electronic surveillance, the U.S. Army and CIA developed a team of remote viewers who used their abilities to analyze hidden targets. The program, known as Stargate, existed from 1973 to 1994. Favorite targets included secret activities in the former Soviet Union. One of the best-known and most-successful remote viewers was Joe

McMoneagle, a chief warrant officer. After Stargate ended, McMoneagle retired and continued remote viewing as a private citizen.

When Rob was writing *The Fog*, about the experience his coauthor Bruce Gernon had in the Bermuda Triangle, he gave McMoneagle several targets to remote view. Gernon had flown through a tunnel in an enormous thunderhead that rendered all his plane's electronic instruments useless. He seemed to leap ahead in time and space.

McMoneagle was given a sealed envelope, labeled Target #2, that contained an illustration depicting Gernon's airplane emerging from a tunnel in the massive storm cloud. A caption below the drawing read: "Exiting the time tunnel vortex. Dec. 4, 1970." A sticky note on the outside of the envelope instructed: "Please describe in detail the target depicted on 12/4/70." All McMoneagle had to go by was the date.

McMoneagle first sensed sound. "Get a strong sense of noise, engine noise, or wind noise, and quick movement, as though moving in a vehicle," he began. "I'm sitting in the left-hand seat and I am male, and my hands are on a steering wheel which is shaped slightly funny."

He called it "a different kind of car, maybe one of those radically different kinds from back in the 70s." He said the driver was wearing headgear, but not a helmet. "It might be some sort of headset for listening to music . . . or some sort of muffler to cut out the loud hissing sounds."

McMoneagle described a complicated dashboard, "cluttered with a lot more equipment than the average automobile." He added, "The driver appears more concerned with the dash panel than watching where he is steering . . . (He) is switching different things on and off. . . . The driver is quite agitated and upset. . . . I have a strong sensation that the loud hissing noises are coming from the headsets and he is trying to change channels on some of the radio equipment, but all he gets is overriding waves of white noise or static."

McMoneagle concluded, "The automobile can't or shouldn't be running. It is anyway, and the driver doesn't appear to be concerned with where he is going, but he does seem more concerned with the system failure. Therefore, it is highly unlikely that this is either an automobile or boat, and much more likely that it is an aircraft."

He went on to say that "the aircraft has entered a very narrow channel of super calm air . . . which contains two very well defined temperature gradients that have slipstreamed together and are polar opposites to the variable temperatures of the aircraft skins. . . . These bi-polar discharges . . . cause the on-board electronics to basically continually reset themselves in a set-loop that appears to be some sort of on-board jamming."

McMoneagle accurately determined that the target was an airplane and that the agitated pilot was dealing with equipment malfunctions under unusual conditions. He also seemed to describe a tunnel—a "narrow channel." He didn't sense any extraordinary movement through time and space—that part of Gernon's experience didn't occur until after he had escaped the tunnel.

Even though the flight took place decades ago and McMoneagle had no knowledge of it, his ability to connect with the experience resulted in synchronicity: a description of an event that resembled the one Rob had in mind. In other words, the internal connected with the external in a way that couldn't be explained by cause and effect.

Empathy and Psychometry

In Secret 2, we wrote about the relationship of emotions and synchronicity. People with empathic abilities, however, take that connection one step beyond. Someone who is "empathic" tunes into the emotions and physical sensations of the person who is being read. Empathy was once described to us as "opening up to the vast, tumultuous ocean of desires, conflicts and pains, triumphs and joys that are specific to the person you're reading."

Psychic Millie Gemondo of West Virginia notes that sometimes the emotional connection to the person she's reading shoves its way into her awareness. While reading for a friend on Florida's west coast, she suddenly felt a pain in her breast and blurted, "You've got a small tumor in your left breast. Get yourself to a doctor immediately." The friend went to the doctor the next day. Sure enough, a small tumor was found and subsequently removed. Millie's warning might've saved her friend's life.

Some empaths hold objects that belong to the person for whom they are reading. This ability, known as psychometry or psychic touch, enables them to read the thoughts that impregnate objects. In other words, it's literally "hands on" psychic power. The term is derived from two Greek words, *psyche*, meaning "the soul," and *metro*, indicating a "measure."

You might've experienced psychic touch yourself when picking up an old object or visiting an ancient site. Some archaeologists have even used talented psychometrists to provide leads for their research of ancient cultures. Psychic detective Johnny Smith, played by actor Anthony Michael Hall, exhibited this ability weekly in the TV series *Dead Zone*. Whenever Smith touched a key object, his visceral reaction played a role in solving a crime or unraveling a mystery.

But it's not all fiction. Renie Wiley, an empath and artist who died in the mid-1990s, often held objects belonging to the person she was reading.

In 1982, Renie and an officer from the Cooper City, Florida, police department were driving near a mall in Hollywood, Florida, where Adam Walsh had last been seen shopping with his mother on July 27, 1981. The cop hoped Renie might be able to pick up something psychically about the missing boy—where he was, what had happened to him, if he'd been abducted. The police suspected he had been kidnapped but didn't have any leads. Renie didn't have an object that had belonged to Adam, but posters of the boy had been plastered across South Florida, his huge, innocent eyes supplicating, begging for help. His face had been burned into the collective consciousness and that seemed to be all Renie needed.

When they were within a few miles of the mall, Renie's hands suddenly flew to her throat. She started choking, gasping for air. The cop had worked with her often enough to understand she was picking up something related to Adam and quickly sped away from the area. After driving several miles, he swerved to the side of the road.

"Adam," she sobbed, "was decapitated."

Not long afterward, the head of the six-year-old boy was found in a field in Vero Beach, more than a hundred miles north of the Hollywood mall.

On a dismal night in the mid-1980s, we accompanied Renie on a case involving a missing girl. Eight-year-old Christie Luna had disappeared near her home in Greenacres, Florida, on May 24, 1984. Around 3:00 P.M., she had walked to a store to buy cat food and never returned. Police suspected foul play.

Renie had requested toys that the missing girl played with, and she sat clutching an old teddy bear. Her eyes were closed. She rocked back and forth, humming softly. Renie was a tall, large-boned woman, yet at that moment everything about her body seemed small and childlike. She started to whimper, then cry, then sob, her body hunched over the teddy bear.

"The mother's boyfriend used to beat up on her," Renie murmured. "She's deaf in one ear because of it." The deafness was later confirmed by the girl's mother.

We left the station and, accompanied by the officer, drove around Greenacres, through the wet darkness. We passed the house where the girl had lived and the store where she was headed when she disappeared. Renie directed us through the streets until we came to a wooded area bordered by a high wire-mesh fence. She didn't like what she felt and turned to the officer. "You should search in there."

Renie felt the girl had been killed by the mother's boyfriend, but the body wasn't found and the case remained unsolved.

Move ahead twenty-four years. Dennie Gooding, a psychic from L.A. with whom we'd both had readings, called to tell us she would be visiting South Florida, where we lived and would be working on a missing person case. She planned to stay with the wife of the cop who had hired her to look into the case. We arranged a time to get together and eventually learned that Dennie was delving into the Christie Luna case.

The police officer who had hired her worked on cold cases for the Palm Beach County sheriff's office. Even though Dennie wasn't able to locate Christie's body, she pinpointed the same wooded area that Renie had—several acres of undeveloped, government-owned land, bordered by a metal fence. "I think she was buried somewhere in there," Dennie said.

The Christie Luna disappearance is tragic, a case that may never be solved unless more information is discovered. For our purpose, the investigations revealed synchronicity. Dennie Gooding and Renie Wiley hit upon the same wooded area where the body could have been buried. Skeptics might say that such a location would be a logical place to hide a body, that logic and cause and effect, rather than synchronicity and psychic ability, were involved. But there's no denying that synchronicity played a role in our involvement. Dennie, who lives three thousand miles away, visited and told us about a cold case we had researched and written about more than two decades earlier. It was as if Christie Luna herself was nudging us all and awaiting justice.

Do You Have the Power of Touch?

You probably have some psychometric abilities, even though you might not realize it. Answer these questions to find out.

- Have you ever sensed someone staring at you, or felt someone's presence in a room before you knew anyone was there?
- Do you get strong feelings, or a flood of emotions and memories, when you look at old photographs?
- When you touch another person or shake someone's hand, do you get impressions about the person's personality?
- Have you ever entered a room and sensed that an argument or other emotionally charged event had just taken place?
- Do you sense other people's moods and adapt to them as if they were your own?

If you answered "yes" to one or more of these questions, you may have some psychometric abilities. The only way to find out is to try it.

PSYCHOMETRY EXERCISE

Start with familiar objects, such as a family member's watch or ring, or maybe a brooch your grandmother wore. If you prefer, use an article of clothing or a letter from a friend.

Find a quiet place where you can relax and clear your mind. Focus on your breathing; take deep, slow breaths. Think positively. Trust your abilities.

Hold the object between your hands. Or, press it to your forehead, to the "third eye." You might find it hard to distinguish what you already know about the person from what you pick up from the object. If you sense something you didn't know about the person, try to find out if it's true.

If you're having trouble getting impressions, don't try so hard. Relax, breathe. As your mind starts to drift, notice stray impressions that touch the edge of your consciousness. Follow whatever it is; see where it takes you.

Next, try objects that belong to people you don't know. See if you get impressions from a folded letter that's not addressed to you and that you haven't read. Or, work with something from the distant past, such as a piece of pottery or an arrowhead. Sometimes you can verify the information you pick up. Other times, you just have to trust your feelings.

Secret 4

THE CREATIVE

Creativity lies at the heart of synchronicity.

"The space between . . . is the space that lies between the observer and the observed; it is the space of the creative act that brings a poem or painting to life."

—F. DAVID PEAT, *PATHWAYS OF CHANCE*

Manifestation is a creative art. As with any other creative endeavor, the more you practice manifestation, the better you become at it. The greater your proficiency, the greater the possibility that synchronicity will coincide with your manifestations. In fact, they may be one and the same.

Think of three objects you would like to see or find today, objects you know will make you feel joyful. Let's say your objects are a rose, a circular gold pendant, and a dragonfly. Spend a few moments concentrating on these objects. See each object vividly in your imagination, holding the image in your mind for at least a minute and a half. While you think about the rose, for example, hold the image until you can see the bright red petals, green thorny stalks, and sharp-edged green leaves. Do the same with the gold pendant and dragonfly.

Then go about your day. If you've visualized vividly, then it's likely you will find each of these objects within a matter of hours, but not necessarily in the way you expect. For example, you may push your shopping cart across the supermarket parking lot and notice a dragonfly hovering above the shrubbery in the median. A few minutes after you get home, the doorbell might ring and a deliveryman hands you a carton containing a dozen red roses. The roses are for a neighbor who isn't home. He asks if you'll give them to her, and as you take them you notice he's wearing a gold pendant around his neck.

It helps if you have a clear reason for selecting an object. During the dead of winter, a woman in Madison, Wisconsin, who hadn't seen the sun for two weeks, wanted very much to see a sunflower during the course of her day. Sunflowers invariably brought her joy and made her think of warmer, more hospitable seasons. Even though the snow was flying, she believed her desire would be manifested. She felt no resistance.

She met her daughter for lunch that day, at a restaurant neither of them had been to before. As she walked in the front door, the first thing she saw was a huge wall poster of a sunflower. Was this experience a synchronicity? Definitely. But it was her strong desire—and the power of her intention and imagination—that brought about the manifestation, through the law of attraction.

The Power of Imagination

In the Harry Potter books and movies, imagination enables the young wizards to travel into those spaces between in order to master some new magical feat. Learning to fly a broom in the Quiddich matches, for example, starts in the imagination. You have to see yourself in your mind's eye flying and controlling the broom. Likewise, when Luke Skywalker is being tutored by Yoda in harnessing the Force, he must first learn to do so in his mind, with his eyes closed. In the movie *Practical Magic*, all the magic begins within.

It's well known that professional athletes enter the zone, the space where they visualize their shots, their plays, and push themselves to the maximum. They see it in as much detail and with as much precision as possible, practicing everything in their heads, *before* they make their moves.

As Coleridge said, "Imagination is the living power and prime agent of all human perception." If we look at creativity as an archetype, it makes perfect sense that when we're in the grips of that archetype, in that powerful flow, we're creating a fertile environment for synchronicity.

Most of us have a creative talent or interest we would like to nurture and develop. But we find all sorts of reasons to procrastinate. We tell ourselves we don't have enough time or money to pursue what we love. Maybe we fear we'll never be able to earn a living doing what we love. But the bottom line is that if you don't try, if you never take the leap of faith and believe in yourself, you'll never know just how creative you are. And if you fail to nurture your creativity, you'll close yourself off to synchronicities that could lead you to the right opportunities and people at the right time.

HOW OPEN ARE YOU?

New experiences are the foundation of any creative process. They help us to see the world and ourselves in new ways. They stimulate new ideas and open us to new possibilities. So before you dive into your creative passion, determine how open you are to new experiences. Read the statements below. Do any of them apply to you?

1. I embrace new experiences.
2. I take risks.
3. Structure is fine, as long as it's not restrictive.
4. I seek excitement in all areas of my life.
5. Routine has its place, but I prefer the unpredictable, the adventurous.
6. When I awake each morning, I'm eager to start my day.
7. I believe I'm a creative person.
8. Whatever I can imagine, I can manifest.
9. I trust the creative process.
10. Whatever I need comes to me.

You get the idea here. These statements are affirmations that help pave the way for your creative self-expression.

Post them on your fridge, your mirror, your office wall.
Mull them over. Say them aloud. Make them come true.
The more you practice such positive affirmations, the more
likely it is that you'll hurl open the doors to synchronicities
that will enable you to achieve whatever you want.

When you bring this sort of awareness to your own creative process, you invite synchronicity into your life, which in turn helps to guide you on your creative path.

Judi Hertling of British Colombia was searching for additional teaching and empowerment tools to help a woman with whom she'd been working. Nothing she'd tried previously seemed right for this particular individual and she was running out of inspiration. A friend who had just finished reading *The Secret* suggested that Judi ask the universe for what she needed. "Like ordering from Costco," she laughed. "Dear Universe, I'd like you to send me the perfect tool for helping someone design a life filled with passion and purpose."

Two weeks later she attended an annual used book sale in support of the SPCA, one of the major book events on Vancouver Island. After three hours of searching through hundreds of books, she was tired and frustrated. She decided to give up and go home. But something at the back of her mind kept nagging at her to check a table of self-help and metaphysical books once more. This time, she found a set of six cassette tapes entitled *Passion, Power, and Purpose*.

"It wasn't until I got home and really looked at my purchase, that I realized the true synchronicity behind what I had bought. Inside, staring up at me from atop the cassettes and the workbook was a large purple sticky note, on which was written in beautiful handwriting: Judith, Thank you for your order. Feel free to order from us again. The universe had indeed provided exactly what I had asked for. Just as if I had ordered it myself."

Such synchronous encounters are what physicist F. David Peat describes as "the human mind operating, for a moment, in its true order and extending throughout society and nature, moving through orders of increasing subtlety, reaching past the source of mind and matter into creativity itself."

Ritual

A ritual is an action performed for its symbolic value. It's used in meditation, visualization, magic, and in religious and spiritual practices. Most creative people also use ritual. A ritual can be something as simple as putting on a certain kind of music or lighting a candle when you sit down to write or paint. Or it can be something as complex as performing a spell to achieve a certain goal.

The first type of ritual is a signal to your muse that you're ready to get to work. It's the equivalent of opening the door to your creative self and becoming a channel for whatever flows through you. It means you are now in a receptive state of mind. The second type of ritual is a form of visualization. Ritual can be a powerful tool for attracting synchronicity and advancing your creative efforts.

When screenwriter Hilary Hemingway sought improvement in her family's finances, she and her husband, writer Jeff Lindsay, went to Key West to perform a prosperity ritual involving an old and prominent ceiba tree near the county courthouse. Featured in the movie *The Fountain*, the ceiba in Mayan cosmology was considered the tree of life that connects earth to sky, or humankind to the divine.

Following the traditional ritual associated with the ceiba, they left a note with their requests at the base of the tree and poured rum around it, symbolically "feeding" the tree—and the muse. Before long, Jeff's novel, *Dexter*, sold in Hollywood and became Showtime's most popular television series. Andy Garcia later took an interest in producing Hilary's script on her uncle Ernest Hemingway's final days in Cuba.

We all have the ability to create new possibilities through our imaginations and intent: ritual is one way of focusing that intent. At every level of creativity—from conception to execution—rituals play a vital role. But it's the nonlocal mind, universal consciousness, that "allows us to imagine beyond the boundaries of what local mind sees as 'possible,' to think 'outside the box,' and to believe in miracles," wrote Deepak Chopra in *The Spontaneous Fulfillment of Desire*.

What kind of rituals do you use in your creative work? Do you have a technique for summoning your muse? Is there a certain time of the day or night when you're most creative? Michael Crichton wrote nearly nonstop once he started a novel. Stephen King puts on rock 'n' roll music and cranks it up loud. Some creative people take walks before they go to work, absorbing the world around them. Julia Cameron advocates journaling, specifically three "morning pages," written by hand, to get into a creative mood for the day. The kinds of rituals you use are unique to you and the type of creative work you do. Once you get into the habit, synchronicity won't be far behind.

Your Muse and Synchronicity

The creative muse speaks to us in many different ways, and synchronicity clearly is one of them. Although we hope the muse will whisper in our ears and dictate the Great American Novel or guide our hands in creating a sculpture that rivals *The Pieta*, the muse works in a subtler manner.

One day in 2001, writer Joyce Evans-Campbell was in a bookstore, browsing the poetry section, and found three collections by Marilyn Taylor, a Wisconsin poet (who in 2008 became that state's Poet Laureate). Joyce bought all three as preparation for a graduate course in poetry she would start the following week. She spent the weekend studying the poems and immersing herself in the poet's style and voice. It would be her first class in graduate school. She didn't have any idea what to expect from the professor, and nervousness about the course eclipsed her excitement.

On Tuesday, the day the course began, Joyce had an MRI that ran longer than expected and walked into the class late. She was surprised to see a woman rather than the male professor listed on the class schedule. She'd hoped to sneak into class without any disruption, but the woman addressed her as she came into class. "Are you Joyce Evans-Campbell?"

Joyce nodded, chastising herself for being tardy on the first day. She took a seat, wondering who the woman was and how she'd known her name. After class, Joyce went up to the professor's desk and apologized for being late. The woman introduced herself. "I'm Marilyn Taylor and I love your columns in the *Journal Sentinel*. I read them all the time."

Joyce was floored. "This encounter established an extraordinary first impression and the two years of study under her went well. That meaningful coincidence opened the door to a deeper relationship and helped me to develop confidence."

The complexity of events that brought about this synchronicity are stunning. When Joyce found Marilyn Taylor's poetry collections in the bookstore, she'd never heard of the poet. She then spent the entire weekend immersing herself in Taylor's work, only to discover that Taylor would be teaching the poetry class because the scheduled professor had died. At any time in this series of events, different decisions might have been made, different paths might have been taken, and the connection might not have happened at all.

In this instance, synchronicity seemed to pull out all the stops, making it possible for Joyce to meet exactly the right creative mentor for that period in her life.

ENGAGING YOUR CREATIVITY

Creative people may be able to tune into that primal soup David Bohm talks about because creativity requires an altered state of consciousness. But all of us are inherently creative, so what we *do* is less important than what we think and feel about what we're doing in any given moment.

When you're looking for an innovative solution or a new way of doing something—at home, in your work, with your children—where do you start? Do you fret and rage, complain and worry? Do you feel anxious? These emotions will only attract more of the same. Instead of railing at the universe because you can't find a solution or feel blocked, take a deep breath. Then send a clear signal to the universe that you want to experience synchronicities related to your concerns. Be passionate about it. Ask for guidance verbally and in writing. Here are some suggestions:

- Create a "magic box" in which to put your request. Display the box prominently. Put flowers or candy around it, if you like.
- Call on your muse. In *On the Craft*, Stephen King wrote about his muse, a guy who lives in the basement and loves loud music. Is your muse male or female?
- Create a wish board with photos, notes, magazine articles, or anything that reminds you of your creative endeavors. Look at it often. Add new material regularly.
- Devise a written plan outlining everything you want to achieve in your creative life for the week, month, year. Update it as needed and keep revising. Look at it frequently. Read it or recite it from heart, and back it with passion.
- Examine your synchronicity notebook for examples that relate specifically to your creative life. In a separate section, write the desired synchronicity like a story with a beginning, a middle, and an end.
- Before going to bed at night, incubate a dream. Tell yourself that you'll have a dream with a message related to your creative endeavors, and more importantly, you'll remember it.

Sometimes synchronicities seem to block rather than guide you. But ultimately you might discover there was a reason your desire didn't work out—and you're probably better off as a result.

Although rejection and disappointment are commonplace in the lives of creative individuals, perseverance wins—defeat must never become an option.

Creativity and Dreams

Some of the most dramatic synchronicities related to creativity occur in and through dreams. And since we spend about a third of our lives asleep, this area deserves closer scrutiny.

In a typical night, you pass through four distinct phases of sleep distinguished by the frequency of brain waves, eye movements, and muscle tension. In the first phase, the brain's rhythms shift from beta—our normal waking consciousness—to alpha, when brain waves oscillate between eight and twelve cycles per seconds. In this stage, you frequently experience hypnogogic images—surreal scenes that usually concern your last thoughts before turning out the light. These brief, psychedelic images can be just as meaningful and synchronistic as longer dreams in the deeper stages of sleep.

In the second phase, the brain registers theta waves, characterized by quick bursts of brain activity. Your eyes flick back and forth beneath your lids. This period of rapid eye movement (REM sleep) usually lasts for several minutes at a time. Most of your dreams occur during this phase, which accounts for up to 25 percent of a night's sleep, or about an hour and a half to two hours for most people. During a normal night, you experience four or five periods of REM sleep. They tend to be short at the beginning of the night and grow progressively longer toward morning, which is why initially it may be easier for you to recall your morning dreams.

The first step in dream recall is easy—get a notebook and pen, preferably one with a light. As you're falling asleep, do so with the intention that you will recall any and all dreams that are relevant to what you're working on or are concerned about. With practice, you'll wake up after relevant dreams and will be able to recall enough to jot down notes. As you become proficient at remembering your last dream of the night, you will learn how to work your way back through each successive dream so that you may be able to recall four or five dreams.

Over time, the lexicon of your dream world will emerge and you'll be able to interpret your dreams with greater ease.

Even nightmares can hold vital clues and answers to your creativity. Elias Howe dreamed that he'd been taken captive by savages who were attacking him with spears that had eye-shaped holes at the end. When he awakened from the nightmare, he realized the dream had given him the final piece of a puzzle for his sewing machine: the eye of the needle belonged near the end of it.

Robert Louis Stevenson struggled for days to find the plot for a new story, then discovered it in a dream, as if it had been handed to him. The result was *The Strange Case of Dr. Jekyll and Mr. Hyde*.

Both men had been deeply immersed in creative and imaginative work that consumed them. When they fell asleep, that intensity bypassed the rational left brain and tapped into what Peat calls "the space between" to find a solution. If they hadn't been able to remember their respective dreams, the development of sewing machines might've been delayed a decade or longer, and Jekyll and Hyde might not have been born! Based on just these two examples, you can see the value of recalling your dreams.

We've kept dreams journals for years and find them extremely helpful. Our dreams have provided us with insights into our own creative processes and with ideas for books—they've even informed us about future sales of our books.

Dreams have also enabled us to break through creative blocks and have alerted us to book sales that were coming up.

Dream Communication

Several years ago, Trish was conducting a workshop at a writers' retreat. As she spoke, she started feeling a level of discomfort that usually portends big trouble with whatever creative project she's working on at the time. Sure enough, by the end of the day, she knew the novel she was writing had collapsed. This is always a depressing moment. Her mind scrambled to patch holes in the plot, to fix the characters. She fell asleep in turmoil and dreamed that her character, Mira Morales, was writing her a letter. Upon awakening, the only lines Trish could recall were: *Don't worry. It'll work out. Much love, Mira.* Trish remembered Mira's advice and was able to rewrite *Black Water*.

The idea for Rob's first novel, *Crystal Skull*, involving the reunion of two ancient crystal skulls, came to him in a dream. After he finished the book, he stumbled across an obscure group called the International Society of Crystal Skulls. He wrote to the organization and received a newsletter that featured an article about the upcoming reunion of two life-sized crystal skulls. Just before leaving for a trip to San Francisco, Rob wrote to Joanne Parks, the owner of one of the skulls, who lived in Houston. En route he was stuck for hours in the Houston airport and upon returning got delayed again and was forced to stay overnight. When he finally arrived home, he received a note from Joanne inviting him to Houston to see Max, her crystal skull.

In this instance, creativity not only attracted synchronicity, but the synchronicity itself brought a new opportunity. Rob's invitation to see the crystal skull finally happened several years after he'd dreamed the plot for his book.

Dreams can provide creative and synchronistic solutions to all sorts of real-life problems. After the death of her great-grandfather, Jennifer Gerard, a businesswoman in Ohio, found some papers in his belongings that detailed the dire straits his family experienced after an economic panic.

He was living with his mother, father, and brother in his grandmother's log house. His grandfather had been dead for years. "We had but little money, one team of horses, a small amount of household goods, and one wagon," Jennifer's great-grandfather wrote. "About midnight on December 23, my brother Wilson woke me up crying. He whispered to me that grandfather had been talking to him about some money. I told him he must be dreaming and to go back to sleep. About five o'clock he woke me up again and said grandfather had returned and that I must get up and do as he said."

The boys slipped out of bed, went into the kitchen, and dressed by the fireplace. Wilson said Grandfather told him there was some money in a box, hidden under the last step of the stairway, over the closet behind their father's bed. Their grandfather wanted the boys to get it and give it to their mother.

They found the box, just as the grandfather in Wilson's dream had instructed. Inside they discovered two buckskin bags filled with silver coins. "Mother burst out crying and the rest of us were soon all weeping with her. After we quieted down, Father and I counted the money. There was $265.00, mostly in French and British coinage, in the two bags. It was certainly a Godsend to us as we had less than $5.00 in the house, and a hard winter ahead."

Creativity and Looking Ahead

Sometimes you may not realize the relationship between a synchronicity and the creative process until long after the creative effort is complete. The mind-blowing case of Edgar Allan Poe and his unfinished sea-adventure novel, *The Narrative of Arthur Gordon Pym*, illustrates just how far into the future creativity can take you.

In the story, three men and a sixteen-year-old boy are adrift at sea in a lifeboat after being shipwrecked. Desperate, on the brink of starvation, they decide to draw lots to determine which of them will be killed and eaten. The cabin boy, Richard Parker, picks the dreaded short straw and is promptly stabbed and consumed.

On July 25, 1884, forty-seven years after Poe stopped working on the novel, a seventeen-year-old cabin boy named Richard Parker was killed and eaten in a similar incident. Parker, on his first voyage on the high seas, boarded the *Mignonette* in Southampton, England, bound for Australia. But when the ship reached the South Atlantic, it was pummeled by a hurricane and sank. The survivors, who had boarded a lifeboat, had few provisions, and after nineteen days adrift they grew desperate. The men discussed drawing lots to choose a victim who would be eaten by the others, but settled on Parker, who had become delirious from drinking seawater. The remaining crew survived on Richard's carcass for another thirty-five days until they were rescued by the SS *Montezuma*, aptly named after the cannibal king of the Aztecs.

The eerie connection between fiction and real life was revealed on May 4, 1974, when twelve-year-old Nigel Parker, a relative of Richard Parker, submitted the story to the *Sunday*

Times of London. The newspaper was conducting a contest to find the best coincidence. The Richard Parker story not only won, but was called one of the best "coincidences" ever recorded by the contest's sponsor, author Arthur Koestler. It also fortified Poe's place in the literary annals of the strange and unusual.

Morgan Robertson's novel *Futility*, published in 1898, offers another fascinating example of creativity, synchronicity, and the future. In it, a supposedly unsinkable ship called the *Titan* strikes an iceberg in the North Atlantic. The fictional story mirrors the sinking of the *Titanic* fourteen years later. Robertson said the idea for his book was inspired by a "vivid trance vision."

Consider these striking similarities:

- The *Titanic* was the world's largest luxury liner—882 feet, displacing 66,000 tons—and was once described as being unsinkable. The *Titan* was the largest craft afloat—800 feet, displacing 75,000 tons—and was considered indestructible.
- The *Titanic* had three propellers and two masts; the *Titan* was equipped with the same.
- Both vessels set sail on their maiden voyages in April. The *Titanic* carried only twenty lifeboats, less than half the number required for the passenger capacity of 3,000. The *Titan* carried "as few as the law allowed," twenty-four lifeboats, less than half needed for her 3,000 passenger capacity. The *Titan* set sail with 2,500 passengers; the *Titanic* left the port with 2,207 passengers.

Compounding the strangeness of these parallels, some months after the *Titanic* sank, a tramp steamer was traveling through the foggy North Atlantic with only a young boy on watch. Suddenly, he sensed the steamer was in the area where the *Titanic* had sunk. Terrified and panic-stricken, he sounded a warning. The ship halted. As the fog began to clear, the passengers on the ship were relieved to see they had stopped just in the nick of time. A huge iceberg loomed ominously in front of them, directly in their path. Incredibly, the name of the steamer was the *Titanian*.

EXERCISE IN CREATING THE FUTURE

If quantum physicists are right and everything in the universe is intimately connected, you can compose a short story linked to a future event. You don't have to be a writer to pursue this exercise. Its purpose is to document a future incident.

Tell yourself that you're going to come up with an idea that will read like headlines from a future date. Think in terms of a few days, weeks, or months. If you write about the distant future, you may not be able to verify it.

Sit down at your computer or with paper and pen. Quiet your mind, relax, and take a few deep breaths. Affirm your intentions. Tell yourself that the creative part of you is not tied to the present but can travel into the future. Don't make up a story that relates to something you heard that might happen in the future. Just let an idea come to you. Jot down details and impressions that come to mind. Don't worry about writing style or punctuation.

If no ideas present themselves, then let it go and try again later. Maybe you can only come up with a couple of lines, not a complete story. That's okay. The idea is to use your creativity to tap into the future. Once you're finished, file what you've written away and keep your eyes open for an event that resembles your story.

Synchronicity as Affirmation

When some part of your life goes south—a relationship, your finances, a job, a business venture—your creativity may seem to dry up. But if you keep seeking innovative solutions, if you keep trying to slog through the morass, synchronicity hums along in the background, an invisible ally. Then, suddenly, connections are made, and the synchronicity that manifests itself in the midst of all the chaos is an affirmation that you're on the right path, making the right decision, doing the right thing. For Gail Provost Stockwell, cofounder of the Writers' Retreat Workshop, a synchronicity kept the retreat—now in its twenty-second year—alive.

In 1987, Gail and her first husband, Gary Provost, started the retreat, a ten-day intensive and immersive workshop for fiction writers. The staff classes are geared specifically to the craft of fiction writing. Visiting authors, editors, and agents are also invited to teach and lecture. Gary passed away suddenly in 1994, but the retreat continued.

By 1998, Gail had remarried and she and her husband, Lance, were struggling to continue the retreats. "Enrollment had dropped, we no longer had a location for the retreat, we didn't have a budget for advertising," Gail says. "It was a real low point. The future of the retreat looked pretty bleak." But they kept reaching out, hoping, following leads, trying different fund-raising venues.

Upon returning from a depressing fund-raising trip, Gail felt things couldn't get any worse. She remembers walking into her house one Saturday morning feeling frustrated and defeated, ready to give up. "Then I went into my office and found more than a hundred messages on the answering machine from people who wanted to know where they could sign up for the retreat." The day before, *USA Today* had run a travel story on ten educational vacations and the Writers Retreat Workshop was mentioned.

To this day, Gail isn't sure how *USA Today* found out about the retreat. But the break arrived just when they needed it, a synchronistic affirmation that the retreat would not only survive, but flourish. Today, the WRW draws students from all over the world. Many of the aspiring writers who have taken the course have been published.

UNLOCKING YOUR CREATIVITY

Sometimes when you're involved in a creative project, you encounter blocks. Your best efforts to move ahead get stymied. Your muse is out to lunch. How do you overcome blockages that seem to separate you from your creative self?

First, think of the creative process as a story. Conflict is inherent in storytelling, and the same is true in your situation. If everything went well from start to finish in a story, you would probably lose interest after a few pages.

Once you accept that occasional blocks are normal, you can use synchronicity to overcome difficulties. Here's one idea: move away from your workplace and listen to what other people are saying, whether they are talking to you or to each other. Or, maybe you hear someone talking on the radio or television. Catch a few phrases. Even if what you hear has nothing to do with your project, give it a chance. Play with the words. Look for hidden hints. How can they apply to your problem?

Just as Rob was writing the above paragraph and wondering how to proceed, Trish called out, "Hey, look at that opossum outside my window." Ironically, seeing an opossum, according to one book on animal symbolism, indicates that you need to dig deeper and look for hidden meaning. That's exactly what Rob was writing about. Looking for hidden meaning. Synchronicity.

Another source on the meaning of opossum gives this suggestion: Show what you know and stop hiding your abilities. That's also good advice for breaking through a block.

Secret 5

THE CLUSTERS

Synchronicity manifests itself in clusters of numbers, names, objects, words, symbols.

"I now have almost as many weird 23s in my files as (Charles) Fort once had records of rains of fish, and people are always sending me new ones."

—ROBERT ANTON WILSON, *FORTEAN TIMES*

Anthony S. Clancy of Dublin, Ireland, was born on the seventh day of the week, seventh day of the month, seventh month of the year, seventh year of the century: 7/7/1907. He was the seventh child of a seventh child, and had seven brothers. On his twenty-seventh birthday, at a race card meeting, he looked at his race card to pick a winner in the seventh race. "The horse numbered 7 was called Seventh Heaven, with a handicap of seven stone. The odds were seven to one." So what did Clancy do? What else? He put seven shillings on the horse . . . and it finished seventh. The Clancy story was in a letter written to Arthur Koestler after *The Roots of Coincidence* was published.

Awakening to Clusters

Clusters of numbers, names, words, phrases, songs, objects, and events are one of the most curious aspects of synchronicity. When it happens, noted Frank Joseph, you invariably feel "that something important, perhaps even divine, is trying to communicate through the numerical symbol."

Jung, who experienced many numerical synchronicities throughout his life, believed that numbers represent "an archetype of order which has become conscious." The meanings of such clusters may not be immediately apparent when you experience them. But by interpreting them as metaphors, by doing some research and using your intuition, you can gain clarity and a deeper appreciation for how your inner self, your unconscious, guides you.

Let's say that for several days you see a cluster of numbers everywhere—on your clock, your microwave, the radio dial, on TV, on bills. These numbers recur with such frequency that you mention it to other people. You begin to feel these numbers are stalking you. Maybe you Google the numbers to learn what, if anything, they mean and discover that other people are experiencing the same thing, with the same numbers. You even find numerous websites and blogs that address these numbers. You might delve into numerology and esoteric texts to uncover the possible message. Suddenly, a whole new world of synchronistic mystery has opened up to you.

Sometimes, the meaning of a number cluster is obvious. If you're seeing your lucky number repeated everywhere, then it's likely that something fortunate is about to transpire. If you're seeing 911 everywhere, perhaps you're being warned about an emergency or crisis in the near future. That's what happened to a man who posted anonymously on our blog. We'll call him John.

For several months in late 2008, John repeatedly glanced at the clock precisely at 9:11. The numbers popped up every time he turned on a TV or radio, and even in conversations. "It became so overwhelmingly evident I had to notice it." Several months after the phenomenon began, his father died, followed a week later by the death of a good friend. And then it stopped. "In all the chaos that followed the deaths, I forgot about it until it started happening again. That's when I realized I was getting 911 calls from the universe."

We've gathered information about some of the most common number clusters and provided various interpretations for them. But just as any synchronicity is meaningful only to the person who experiences it, so is the significance of a particular cluster of numbers unique for each individual. Use these meanings and stories as springboards for your own exploration.

11, 111, and 11:11

If you Google 11:11, about 200 million sites come up. Obviously, there's considerable interest in these numbers, and this cluster is among the most common. Even MSNBC commentator Keith Olbermann experienced one of these clusters.

On bat night at Yankee Stadium in April 2009, Yankee Brett Gardner swung at a pitch. His bat slipped from his hands, flew into the stands, and struck a boy named Jacob Smith. Bat night, indeed. Smith is Olbermann's nephew. Nine years earlier, Yankee second baseman Chuck Knoblauch threw wildly to first base. The ball bounced off the roof of the dugout and struck Marie Olbermann, Keith's mother, in the face. Olbermann was a sportscaster, covering baseball for Fox News at the time. Knoblauch and Gardner both wore number 11.

Here are some intriguing historical synchronicities involving number 11:

- The WWI armistice was signed at 11:11 A.M. on 11/11/18.
- World War II ended on the 11th hour of the 11th day of the 11th month.
- Yasser Arafat died on 11/11/04.
- JFK was assassinated on 11/22.
- Supposedly, the Mayan calendar ends at 11:11 universal time, in 2012.
- The U.S. Navy lists the 2012 solstice for 12/21/12 at 11:11 universal time.

Uri Geller, the famed Israeli psychic, devotes a large section on his website to 11:11. He claims he started experiencing the 11:11 phenomenon in 1986. The incidents proliferated and he began noticing the numbers on computers, microwave ovens, cars, documents, and hotel rooms. When he decided to write about it on his website, he was flooded with e-mail from people who were also experiencing the 11:11 phenomenon. Geller's website explains this at great length, but essentially says 11:11 is a doorway, "a crack between two worlds . . . a bridge which has the inherent potential of linking together two very different spirals of energy."

According to a book called *11:11: Inside the Doorway*, the numbers 11:11 tend to occur during periods of heightened awareness. They reactivate "cellular memory banks" and act as verification that we're on the right path.

Other esoteric meanings? You're being ushered into a greater reality, shown how to separate yourself from illusion, moving closer to "spirit" or to an "ET consciousness." The trouble with some esoteric interpretations is they sound like fringe stuff. That doesn't mean they're invalid, but to you the appearance of these numbers might indicate something more ordinary.

Confirmations and warnings also seem to accompany this cluster. On a website called Celestine Vision, based on the bestselling book *The Celestine Prophecy*, a message board about synchronicity defines 111 or 1111 as "Energy flow of water, money, sex, kundalini, magnetic. It happens when one of these energies manifests."

While writing this section, we received a bill from Megan's college for the year-end cleaning of the dorm suite she shared with three other women. The charge? $111 and change. It certainly indicated a flow of money, but the money was going out, not coming in.

The same day, we were writing the first draft of this chapter and corresponding with people on our blog about the

11:11 phenomenon. We took a break so Rob could pick up our Mazda, which had just gotten its second alternator in two weeks. As he drove away from the garage at 3:17 P.M., he looked down at the clock. Because the battery had been disconnected the clock had stopped. It read 11:11.

The meaning you relate to this number cluster, or any cluster, could be determined by your age, family background, culture, and, of course, your present circumstances. One day, Jenean Gilstrap from Delaware was in the car with her seventeen-year-old grandson, Christopher, when he looked at his cell phone and suddenly gasped, "Oh, Nanny, look, it's exactly eleven. I have to make a wish!" Jenean, curious about his perception of the number's significance, asked what he meant. "Don't you know? That's a magical number!"

Author Nancy Pickard, whose novel *Virgin of Small Plains* was voted the 2009 title for Kansas Reads, dropped us an e-mail in the spring of 2009 to let us know she had just finished a tour of 11 libraries, in 11 towns, in 11 days. "I guess I'm doing exactly what I'm supposed to be doing." In both instances, the people involved viewed the cluster as something positive.

Jeff D'Antonio, a high school physics teacher, had read our post on 11s. The next day when he was out running errands, listening to the radio in the car, a song from the 1980s came on—"Domino" by Genesis—about nuclear war, the domino effect. "The first domino falls, setting off an unstoppable chain of events—think Cold War, mutual assured destruction, all those concepts we heard so much about back in the eighties. When the song came on, I happened to look at my watch. It was 11:11:11. All those ones look a lot like dominos lined up, waiting for the first one to fall, don't they?"

Once we're aware of number clusters, do we tend to see them more frequently? Or are we being offered a glimpse into the internal symmetry and order of the universe? Pythagoras, the Greek scientist, mathematician, and priest who lived around 500 B.C., thought the latter was true. He believed numbers constituted the very fabric of the universe. For Jung, the number 1 was more than a number. In *Memories, Dreams, Reflections* he referred to it as unity. "But it is also 'the unity,' the One, All-Oneness, individuality and non-duality—not a numeral but a philosophical concept, an archetype and the attribute of God, the monad."

Heady stuff. Whether we refer to these cluster synchronicities of 11s as "stalkers," wake-up calls, or as integral to a spiritual journey, it's safe to say that people who experience them sit up, take notice, and, ultimately, may be changed by what they discover.

As writer Terri Patrick remarked on our blog, the message of 11:11 is about illumination and enlightenment. "From what I've seen, anyone who pays attention to repetitive numbers usually begins a journey to determine the meaning of these numbers." Interestingly, her comment was the eleventh one under an entry entitled #11, and it was sent during the eleventh hour of the evening.

3, 33

Clusters of 3s also attract attention. Esoterically, three represents the trinity of body, mind, and spirit, intuition and right-brain thinking, spirituality, creativity, the archetypes of mother, father, and child, and the Holy Trinity. When you experience clusters of 3s, any of these esoteric meanings might apply, but as with any synchronicity, you are the best interpreter of the experience. Sometimes the interpretation may require some research.

During a flight to California, we noticed the number 33 kept cropping up. Aisle 33, seat 33, flight 233. In a period of about seven hours, we noted half a dozen recurrences of the number. We didn't have any idea what it meant. Trish finally turned to the *I Ching*—an ancient Chinese oracle that consists of sixty-four patterns called hexagrams—and looked up hexagram 33. As soon as she saw the title—Retreat—she understood the message.

At the time, her mother was in an Alzheimer's unit, in room 33. We were in "retreat" from that situation. We interpreted the synchronicity as confirmation we had made the right choice in taking a break. But the numbers were meaningful only to us.

For NASCAR driver Kevin Harvick, 33 had an entirely different meaning. In March 2009, he mastered the half-mile oval track with steep inclines in the heart of the Tennessee mountains and won at Bristol Motor Speedway. He was driving car 33, was thirty-three years old, and it was his thirty-third race. If you look at the date of his win—3/21/09—you can easily extrapolate two more 33s. Add 2 and 1 and it's 3/3 or 33. And the year 09 is 3 times 3, another 33.

Ray Getzinger, whose story about the redheaded girl is included in Secret 3, wrote that when he was reading the post about 11:11 he zeroed in on a comment someone had left about awakening at 3:33 every morning. "I remembered an episode of *CSI: NY* in which Lt. Taylor wakes up at 3:33 every morning. Then yesterday morning I woke up at 3:33 A.M."

In some instances, awareness of certain numbers seems to initiate our own experiences.

YOUR NUMBER CLUSTERS

Whenever you experience a synchronicity of number clusters, jot down what was happening at the time. Note your mood, emotions, who was with you, all the circumstantial details. Over time, a pattern should emerge. You may discover the clusters tend to appear at certain periods of the day—at night, for instance, or when you're driving or in a relaxed state.

Let's say that in the space of several hours, you experience a cluster of 8s. Your grocery store bill was $88.08, your lunch cost exactly $8.88, and you received your mortgage bill for $888.88. To decipher the message, begin with what the number 8 means to you. Is it your lucky number? With what do you associate it? Have you experienced sequences of 8 before? If so, what were the circumstances? If nothing comes to mind, research the number. Study its esoteric symbolism and see if something resonates. Sometimes, the appearance of a cluster of numbers encourages awareness, awakening you to the mysteries of the universe.

The 27 Club

Once you become aware of synchronicities involving numbers, they seem to occur everywhere. One evening, we were in the kitchen preparing dinner while Megan was in the living room, watching a Hollywood story about Kurt Cobain. We were sort of half-listening. We knew that Cobain was a suicide but didn't realize that he—like fellow musicians Jimi Hendrix, Janis Joplin, Jim Morrison, and Brian Jones—died at age twenty-seven.

Charles R. Cross, the biographer of both Cobain and Hendrix, wrote that the number of musicians who died at age twenty-seven is "truly remarkable by any standard." A music website, the 27 Club, lists thirty-four musicians who died at age twenty-seven, dating back as far as 1892.

According to numerology, if you add the digits in 27, 2 + 7, you get 9, the number of beginnings and endings. We wondered about that. The next afternoon, Rob picked up *Synchronicity & You,* by Frank Joseph and it fell open to pages 28–29. Here's what Rob read about the number nine. "Among some musicians it is regarded as death's own number. This negative association began with Beethoven, who died after completing his ninth symphony."

If you experience clusters with 27 and you are twenty-seven or younger, don't immediately jump to the conclusion that you're going to die at that age. This particular meaning is just one of many. In certain traditions, 27 represents the "divine light" and has absolutely no connection to death.

If 27 is repeated in your environment—for instance, your birth date, the birth dates of people around you, your home address, pivotal events that occurred at that age, digits in your phone number—you may wish to research this number. On one website, a single individual recorded more than 300 occurrences of the number 27 in his life. That kind of pattern—involving 27 or any other number—could hint at some deeper issue, even a pattern brought from a past life.

14

Number clusters range from the odd to the truly strange. They can coalesce around a single event or continue over the course of a lifetime. For Maria, a college sophomore, the number 14 occurred four times in as many months.

One night she drove into a DUI checkpoint on her way to McDonald's. Earlier that evening, she'd drunk two beers. After performing the field sobriety tests, the policeman determined she was impaired, arrested her, and administered the Breathalyzer test. Even though Maria blew under the legal limit for impairment, she spent fourteen hours in jail before she was bailed out.

Her parents hired an attorney, who felt she had a strong case for dismissal based on the video of her field sobriety tests and because she blew under the legal limit. After reviewing the evidence, the prosecutor was ready to dismiss the charges, but he was removed from the case. Another prosecutor was assigned, who proceeded with charges, and Maria's court date was set for December. Because it fell during final exam week, the attorney asked for a continuance and a new court date was set for February.

Before Christmas, fourteen law firms filed a motion that the DUI checkpoints in that particular county were illegal because the police had too much discretion. The motion was heard on January 14, and the judged ruled in favor. All the evidence was dismissed in fourteen cases, including Maria's. 14 hours, 14 law firms, January 14 and 14 cases.

Perhaps the number 14 is Maria's new lucky number. In numerology, the digits in 14 add up to 5, the number associated with freedom. Another connection: the name Maria contains five letters, and the letters in her full name, when converted to numerological equivalents, equal 5. Not only was Maria set free of the charges, but on the night of the incident, she had broken up with her boyfriend because she wanted more freedom. She feels she attracted the experience so she would gain a deeper appreciation for her freedom.

23

This number looks innocuous enough, but when you begin to dig around, some of the correlations and synchronicities are just plain weird. Let's start with literature.

Shakespeare was born on April 23, 1564 and died on April 23, 1616. His first folio was published in 1623.

In Tangiers in the early 1960s, William Burroughs, author of *Naked Lunch*, knew a certain Captain Clark who ran a ferry from Tangiers to Spain. Clark boasted he'd been running the ferry for twenty-three years without an accident. That same day, the ferry sank, killing Clark and everyone aboard. That very evening, as Burroughs was ruminating about this gruesome event, he turned on the radio and heard about the crash of a New York–Miami airplane. The plane was piloted by a Captain Clark. It was Flight 23.

This synchronicity apparently shocked Burroughs enough that he began compiling a list of synchronicities involving the number 23. In 1965, his friend and fellow author Robert Anton Wilson also began putting together a list of oddities about the number. One of the personal synchronicities he noted concerned his daughters, born August 23 and February 23. Wilson wrote about the number for the *Fortean Times* in 1977; his article appeared in issue 23.

Hollywood has its share of 23s, too. Take *The X-Files*'s production company, Ten-Thirteen. The numbers 10 and 13 add up to 23. The show's creator, Chris Carter, was born on 10/13. Fans of *The X-Files* might remember an abandoned nuclear silo where a UFO was being held. The number 1013 appeared on the side of the silo. In another episode, Mulder went to the apartment of a recently deceased man; the number 23 was on the door.

In the TV series *Lost*, which builds on layers of synchronicity, many oddities involve 23.

- Oceanic Flight 815: 8 + 15 = 23
- The flight departed from gate 23
- Jack's seat on the plane was 23A
- Rose and Bernard were sitting in row 23
- Hurley stayed in a Sydney hotel on floor 23
- The reward for turning Kate in: $23,000
- One of the numbers in the sequence of six that won Hurley the lottery and opened the hatch was 23: 4 8 15 16 23 42

Even if the repetition of 23s in the series is intentional, it's nonetheless the sort of weirdness that would have interested both Burroughs and Wilson.

In 2007, a Jim Carrey movie, *The Number 23*, met with lukewarm reviews, but the premise is intriguing. Walter Sparrow, an amiable dogcatcher, becomes obsessed with a murder mystery novel that continually circles the number 23. The people in the book who become obsessed with the number 23 invariably end up dead. Carrey's character believes the story parallels his own life and that the author is writing about him.

Burroughs and Wilson saw 23 primarily as a death number. They may have been onto something. The twenty-third Psalm is a popular reading at funerals. Burroughs discovered that the bootlegger Dutch Schultz had Vincent "Mad Dog" Coll assassinated on 23rd Street in New York when Coll was twenty-three years old. Schultz himself was assassinated on

October 23. Wilson dug a bit deeper and discovered that Charlie Workman, the man convicted of shooting Schultz, served twenty-three years of a life sentence before being paroled. Wilson noted that in telegraphers' code, 23 means "bust" or "break the line." Hexagram 23 in the *I Ching* means "breaking apart." In Charles Dickens's *A Tale of Two Cities*, the twenty-third man, Sidney Carlton, is guillotined in the final scene. In *The Wrestler*, Mickey Rourke, playing an over-the-hill wrestler heading toward his final match and possibly his death, has the number 23 boldly scrawled on the wrappings around his leg.

What about science and math? Here, too, 23 proves intriguing.

- During conception, each parent contributes twenty-three chromosomes to the fetus.
- Euclid's geometry has twenty-three axioms.
- Twenty-three is the first prime number in which both digits are prime numbers and add up to another prime number.
- It takes twenty-three seconds for blood to circulate through the human body.
- Every twenty-third wave that slams into a shore is twice as large as the average wave.
- The first lunar landing was in the Sea of Tranquility, 23.63 degrees east. The second lunar landing was in the Ocean of Storms, 23.42 degrees west. The first two landing missions were Apollo 11 and Apollo 12; 11 + 12 = 23.
- The earth rotates completely every 23 hours, 56 minutes.
- The axis of the earth is 23.5 degrees.
- Humans have a physical biorhythm cycle of twenty-three days.

- The pattern of DNA shows irregular connections at every twenty-third section.
- Humans have twenty-three vertebrae running down the main part of their spines.
- The Harmonic Convergence occurs every 23,000 years.
- Geosynchronous orbit occurs at 23,000 miles above earth's surface.
- The fall equinox usually occurs on September 23.
- W is the twenty-third letter in the alphabet. Numerologically, WWW, the World Wide Web, translates as 23 + 23 + 23.

Again, we want to stress that experiencing synchronicity clusters with the number 23 doesn't mean you're going to die, that you're cursed, or anything else of that nature. But it could mean you're going through a major transformative period in your life. The repetition of this number may indicate a path you haven't recognized yet.

137

This sequence and everything associated with it is baffling, mysterious. If this number recurs for you, it deserves close scrutiny.

Wolfgang Pauli, an early supporter of Jung's theory on synchronicity, was confounded by one of the unsolved mysteries of modern physics: the value of the fine structure constant, which involves the number 137.

A prime number can be divided only by 1 and by itself. Or, put another way, a prime number is a positive integer that cannot equal the product of two smaller integers. That makes 137 a prime number and a particularly baffling one. In *Deciphering the Cosmic Number: The Strange Friendship of Wolfgang Pauli and Carl Jung*, Arthur I. Miller provides a brief but fascinating history of the number 137 in the world of quantum physics.

It was "discovered" in 1915 by Arnold Sommerfield, Pauli's mentor when he was still a student. "From the moment 137 first popped up in his equations, he and other physicists . . . quickly realized that this unique 'fingerprint' was the sum of certain fundamental constants of nature, specific quantities believed to be invariable throughout the universe, quantities central to relativity and quantum theory."

The number became so baffling to physicists that the great Richard Feynman, who won the Nobel Prize in 1965 for his contributions to the development of quantum electrodynamics, said physicists should put a sign in their offices to remind themselves of how much they don't know. The sign would be simple: 137.

Not only is 137 "the DNA of light," as Miller puts it, but it is also the number associated with the *Kabbalah*. Miller explains that in ancient Hebrew, numbers were written with letters, and each letter had a number associated with it. The system sounds very much like numerology. "Adepts of the philosophical system known as the *Gematria* add the numbers in Hebrew words and thus find hidden meanings in them." In Hebrew, the word *Kabbalah* has four letters that add up to 137. Not surprisingly, physicists began referring to 137 as a mystical number.

Pauli certainly found this to be the case. He wrestled with its implications most of his life. When he was admitted to the hospital at the age of fifty-eight and learned he would be in room 137, he supposedly said, "I will never get out of here." He was right. He died shortly thereafter.

F. David Peat had his own experience with number 137 when he visited the Jung Institute in Bollingen, Switzerland. In an e-mail to us, he explained he was invited to give a lecture to celebrate the institute's fiftieth year. Upon arrival at the hotel next to the institute, he was given a key and told his room was on the second floor of the annex. Before going to his room, he walked down to the lake "to get something of the spirit of Jung." But after thirty minutes, nothing happened, so Peat decided to return to the hotel, sleep, and perhaps have a dream about Jung. "I took the elevator to the second floor, removed the key from my pocket and it was 137! I realized I was there to talk about Pauli, not Jung."

That evening, Peat told the story about the key and an old man at the back of the room laughed. "Later when I wrote an equation on the board, the same old man said, 'It won't work.'"

At the reception, Peat asked who the old man was. He turned out to be an assistant who was with Pauli in the hospital in room 137.

Pauli recognized the number 137 as the archetype of death. Peat recognized it as Pauli's calling card. As Frank Joseph wrote in *Synchronicity & You*, "the recipient of synchronicity is its best interpreter. To anyone else, the 137 would have meant nothing."

Even Hollywood has used 137. In *FlashForward*, a show that premiered on ABC in the fall of 2009, the seven billion people living on the planet black out at the same moment, for 137 seconds, and live a scene from their individual futures. Why that number? It will be interesting to see where the writers take this show.

Other Types of Clusters

Some people never experience synchronicities involving number clusters. But they experience clusters of names, phrases, places, even dates. If you fall into this category, get into the habit of writing down the conditions and your mood at the time of the experience. Also, make note of the date and time of day the synchronicity occurred.

Synchronistic clusters involving names, phrases, places, and/or dates may be addressing:

1. An event, situation, or relationship that will unfold in the future
2. A deeper issue or belief that is holding you back or restricting you in some way
3. A project, relationship, situation, or event happening in your life now
4. Camaraderie you share or will share with another person
5. The deeper connections you have to the larger world
6. People who are in your life now or will be in the near future
7. Something not included in this list

Always keep in mind that synchronicity is first and foremost something meaningful to you. Other people might acknowledge how curious it is that you experience these recurring names or objects, but the meaning is yours and yours alone.

When clusters involve names or words, research their etymology. There could be a message in the root of the word or name. Are these clusters recurring themes in your life? Try to interpret them as metaphors, just as you might interpret a dream.

- Note the source. A dream? Words of a song? Images on TV or in magazines?
- How often are they repeated—within minutes, days, weeks? Do they disappear for a while, then start again?
- Watch for patterns. Correlate the cluster patterns to events occurring in your life or in the lives of people to whom you're close.
- Dig around and make associations to find the meaning. Sometimes the meaning isn't obvious until some time passes and other events occur. The point is to identify clusters, find meaning; insight, and information; and see how you can utilize it.

Clusters of Names, Phrases, Places, Dates

In his book on synchronicity, *Synchronicity: An Acausal Connecting Principle*, Jung mentions a personal experience that involved a fish motif, which turned up six times within twenty-four hours.

On April 1, 1949, Jung made a note about an inscription that involved a fish. At lunch, he and his family ate fish. In some European countries at that time, April 1 was known as "Fish Day" and during lunch someone mentioned making an "April fish." That same afternoon, a former patient he hadn't seen for months showed him some paintings she had done of fish. That evening, someone showed Jung a piece of embroidery with fish-like sea monsters stitched into it. The next morning, a patient he hadn't seen for years related a dream she'd had about a fish.

At the time this cluster of synchronicities occurred, Jung was researching the fish symbol in history and noted that fish often represent unconscious contents. "This run of events made a considerable impression on me," Jung wrote. "It seemed to me to have a certain numinous quality."

This "numinous quality" is a characteristic many people mention when talking about their synchronicities. It's as if the hand of the cosmos sweeps into our lives and shakes things up magically so that we no longer see the world or ourselves in the same way. To Jung, synchronicity was evidence of a unitary reality he termed *unus mundus*, an alchemical expression that means one world. So, even the simplest synchronicity, such as thinking about eggs and someone on television says "eggs," can fill us with a sense of the magic and wonder inherent in the universe. In more contemporary terms, the *unus mundus* might be called the Law of Attraction, popularized in *The Secret*.

This sense of wonder was certainly true when we experienced the repetition of the name Max. Within minutes of posting a synchronicity on our blog by someone calling himself Max Action, a friend sent an e-mail about an exhibit in Miami featuring Max, one of the legendary crystal skulls. An hour later, at the beginning of Rob's yoga class, Trish asked the guy next to her if he and his wife would be interested in adopting one of the stray cats we were feeding. He sort of chuckled and said, "We can't do cats. Max would eat it whole." Max is his dog.

These types of synchronicities aren't paradigm busters, but clusters invariably grab our attention. And when we pay attention, we're better able to decipher what the ancients called "miracles of the gods." Meaningful coincidence, wrote Alan Vaughan in *Patterns of Prophecy*, "is the result of—and evidence of—a divinity that organizes all creation through the operation of archetypes."

SIMULTANEOUS DISCOVERIES

Simultaneous discoveries, such as the independent discovery of calculus by both Sir Isaac Newton and Gottfried Leibniz, and the theory of evolution by Charles Darwin and Alfred Russell Wallace, are another type of cluster. "Do such concepts and insights exist in some enfolded, symbolic form within the unconscious mind?" wondered F. David Peat in *Synchronicity: The Bridge Between Matter and Mind*. "Or are they approached within nature, not directly but in some hidden way which must be unfolded within the languages of art, literature, music, or science?"

Jung, too, saw synchronicity as the reason independent researchers can come up with the same results or knowledge at the same time. Congealing in the unconscious is the need for answers. Searching for a solution in their own ways, researchers resolve the problem simultaneously.

Peat further points out that some synchronicities could involve "becoming linked with the environment in a special way, anticipating events or sensing some underlying pattern to the world."

Clusters even occur with birth dates and astrological signs, sometimes in the most unexpected places. Author and past-life researcher Carol Bowman was visiting her mother in New York's Hudson Valley area. Small town. Not much there. She'd gone to the grocery store for basics. While waiting in line, she noticed the Asian woman behind her had a toddler in her cart, a cute little girl. Carol asked the woman how old her daughter was.

Asian woman: "She'll be two next month. She's an Aries."

Carol: "My Aries daughter will be thirty next month. Aries kids are a handful, aren't they?"

Asian woman, laughing: "That's for sure. And I'm married to an Aries."

Carol's antenna twitched. "Me, too!"

So we can imagine these two women in line at this dinky store, suddenly aware of some sort of connection, both with Aries daughters, both married to Aries men. Carol then asks, "What sign are you?"

Asian woman: "I'm a Libra."

Carol understood that something odd and fascinating was happening. "I'm a Libra too. What's your birth date?"

Asian woman: "October 14."

"That's, uh, my birth date, too."

Sounds like a scene out of an episode of *The Twilight Zone*. You can almost hear the eerie music—de-de, de-de, de-de, de-de—playing in the back of Carol's mind. She pulled out her business card. "I'll be conducting a past-life workshop here in June. I hope you'll come."

What began as a simple, mundane trip to the grocery store was transformed into something magical. Beneath the veneer of our daily lives lies a deeper order of existence that synchronicity enables us to glimpse. We feel awed, astounded, shocked, or may realize our beliefs are flawed.

Even for people who are familiar with synchronicity and experience it frequently, each instance is a gift. Screenwriter Julian Winter says he "gets nervous" when he doesn't see synchronicity around him. Vivian Ortiz, a psychiatric ER nurse in Savannah, Georgia, is particularly attuned to animal synchronicities and follows guidance about her own pets from these "glimpses into the cosmos." Screenwriter Julie Scully is led to new ideas and screenwriting projects through synchronicities that happen to her frequently in bookstores. When synchronicities occur in the course of our daily lives, we tend to feel we're on the right track, in the groove, exactly where we're supposed to be on our journey through life.

Attunement

When you're attuned to your own psyche, it's easier to create a fertile environment for synchronicity. One day in June, Jenean Gilstrap awakened and wondered how her 6/6/09 day would go. To her, there was something magical and mysterious about these numbers. As she drove to the beach about fifteen miles from her home, she glanced at the license tag of the car passing her in the left lane. The tag had a 222 sequence. The next car's plate had a 444 and the third car an 888. "I almost laughed out loud and wondered where the 666 was and how perfect *that* would be. Then a black Cadillac cruised past and yes, its tags had the missing 666 to complete my little numerical cycle." Here's how Jenean's number breaks down numerologically.

222 = 6
444 = 12 = 3
888 = 24 = 6
666 = 18 = 9

While the 444 doesn't fit with 6/6/09, it equals a 3, which divides each of the others evenly, and it also follows the progression of three-digit numbers.

FINE-TUNING YOUR INTUITION

When you start your day, select a question regarding an issue or concern that's important to you at the time. Then request that some sort of cluster appear during the day, that you'll be able to relate it to your question, and that it will illuminate your concern or issue.

Maybe your boyfriend has seemed distracted lately, and because it's your birthday, you wonder if he's even going to get you a present. During the day, you encounter a clerk whose nametag says Kate. You hear someone on the car radio say Kate, and you see a trailer for a movie starring Kate Hudson.

It's a common name. Maybe it doesn't mean anything, but when you see your boyfriend that evening, you ask him, "Who's Kate?" To your surprise, he answers, "How did you find out about her?" For a moment, you think he's going to break up with you in favor of someone named Kate. To your relief and surprise, he leads you to his car and shows you your birthday present: a kitten he calls Kate-Cat.

Secret 6

THE TRICKSTER

A synchronicity can reveal itself with a twist of humor or wry irony so startling it stops us in our tracks.

"Synchronicities are the jokers in nature's pack of cards for they refuse to play by the rules and offer a hint that, in our quest for certainty about the universe, we have ignored some vital clues."

—F. DAVID PEAT, *SYNCHRONICITY: THE BRIDGE BETWEEN MATTER AND MIND*

The dictionary defines trickster as a cheat, fraud, or deceiver; a person who plays tricks; a supernatural figure appearing in various guises and typically engaging in mischievous activities, important in the folklore and mythology of primitive people and usually conceived as a cultural hero. To these definitions, we would add that the trickster often appears to remind us not to take ourselves so seriously.

The classic trickster synchronicity begins with . . . well, plum pudding. In 1805, French writer Emile Deschamps was treated to some plum pudding by Monsieur de Fontgibu. Ten years later, Deschamps encountered plum pudding on the menu of a Paris restaurant, and wanted to order some, but the waiter told him the last dish had already been served to another customer, who turned out to be Monsieur de Fontgibu. In 1832, Deschamps visited another restaurant with a friend and once again ordered plum pudding. He recalled the earlier incidents and told his friend the only thing missing that would make the setting complete was Monsieur de Fontgibu. At that moment, a senile Monsieur de Fontgibu entered the room by mistake.

Plum pudding became an archetypal connection between the two men—the only connection. The fact that it continued over the course of twenty-seven years, even when one of the men became too senile to understand what was going on, qualifies this story as a double trickster synchronicity.

Writing about this case in *Synchronicity: Science, Myth, and the Trickster*, Allan Combs and Mark Holland suggested that "one gets the sense of a clown or trickster standing behind the scenes, the mythic face of a mischievous god, dimly seen, looking from behind the shroud of coincidence."

Who is this trickster, exactly? What's his message?

The Joker Laughs at You

In *Lord of the Rings*, the sneaky, lurking Gollum character, Smé-agol, is the perfect example of the trickster archetype. He usually had a private agenda of one kind or another that prompted him to mislead the hobbits (or hobbitses, as he called them) on numerous occasions and to trick them into believing he could be trusted.

Archetypes—the trickster, the wise old man or woman, the hero, the child, mother and father—are as ancient as the planet. They bubble into the conscious mind from the collective unconscious, a repository of images common to all people. They're found in mythology, folklore, fairy tales, legends, hallucinations, fantasies, most divination systems, and in dreams.

One of the best-known trickster myths features the Norwegian god, Loki, the son of two giants. He possessed great ingenuity but was a rascal and raconteur who enjoyed stirring up trouble. A shape-shifter who took various forms—including a horse, falcon, and fly—Loki could even change his gender, so it's no wonder trickster synchronicities appear in many guises.

Loki hung out with the major gods, Odin and Thor, yet he was often their enemy. When he wasn't invited to a banquet at Valhalla, for instance, he crashed the party, becoming the thirteenth guest. He lumbered around, demanding food and alcohol, embarrassing everyone. He even tricked Hoder, the blind god of darkness, into shooting Balder, the god of light and joy, with a mistletoe-tipped arrow. Balder died and the earth was plunged into darkness. Ever since, the number thirteen has been considered unlucky.

The myth inspired the Jim Carrey movie *The Mask*. To refresh your memory, Carrey plays a boring bank clerk named Stanley

Ipkiss who discovers a mysterious, ancient, green wooden mask inhabited by Loki. When he puts on the mask, he becomes a manic, green-skinned superhero who does wacky things.

In Native American mythology, the coyote is often depicted as a trickster. He's cunning, adaptable, a shape-shifter who uses his mischievousness to drive home a point and make people laugh. In the young adult novel *Gone*, the author uses coyotes to illustrate their adaptability in a world where everyone over the age of fifteen has mysteriously vanished. In a collection of short stories titled *The Coyote Road Trickster Tales*, the trickster archetype is explored through many different venues: a spirit decides it will do everything possible to stop a classroom from diagramming sentences; a boy draws inspiration from Brer Rabbit to outsmart his kidnappers; and a girl collects ghosts on ribbons and takes them wherever she goes, feeding them her blood.

One of the most recognizable tricksters in mythology is Kokopelli, the humpbacked flutist. Among the Anasazi, Hopi, and Zuni, he was considered the deity of fertility, music, dance, replenishment, and mischief. Overall, he appears far more benevolent than Loki, who became more malicious and mean-spirited as he aged.

Across many cultures, the trickster appears in diverse forms. In popular American culture, he's most readily found in movies. The Joker in the *Batman* series depicts the shadow side of the trickster, more like the aging Loki. One of the most bizarre incarnations of the trickster is Captain Jack Sparrow in *Pirates of the Caribbean*, played by actor Johnny Depp. Sparrow is a ghost capable of great tricks and mischievousness. And yes, he's also a hero.

Indiana Jones and Hans Solo are perfect examples of the union of two archetypes, trickster and hero. The fact that Harrison Ford plays both characters so well suggests the archetype is alive and well within Ford himself.

The trickster is both absurdly human and divinely inspired—a mixture of clown and cultural hero. As a result, trickster synchronicities inspire awe, astonishment, even shock. They can prompt you to re-evaluate relationships, consider alternative career paths, and make choices you might not have considered otherwise. Nearly always, you initially feel as if you're the brunt of the universe's joke. The trick with the trickster is to dig beneath the joke to discover what's really going on, which is often difficult to figure out.

For example, let's say your sweetheart breaks up with you, and as you're listening to the explanation, a bird flies by and craps on your head. It's the perfect punctuation mark, bearing witness to how you feel you've been treated. And it's a trickster synchronicity.

The trickster's scenarios are sometimes complex and startling. Some years ago, Rob was driving a couple of friends, George and Hanna, to the Miami airport. George (a minister for a free-wheeling New Age church in Negril, Jamaica) and Hanna, his Norwegian girlfriend, had known Rob before he'd gotten involved in the ministry. Rob was going through a separation from his first wife, a major life transition that undoubtedly contributed to the intensity of the conversation. They were discussing deep stuff, spiritual belief systems and cosmic questions. Zen. As in the zen of the moment, the zen of peace, the zen of meditation.

Suddenly, Rob noticed the license plate of a passing car. It read: ZEN 665. George blurted, "It would be really remarkable if we saw ZEN 666."

A few minutes later, a yellow sports car passed them with that very license plate: ZEN 666. It was as if the trickster was in the car with them, laughing at their astonishment. They asked for it and it appeared. It was a revelation, as in the source of the number's notoriety: the biblical book of Revelation.

For months, Rob told the story of ZEN 666 repeatedly. He couldn't seem to get over it, and wanted other people to consider the odds of such an incident happening. Several years later, while driving on a street near home, a red sedan passed him bearing the same combination of letters and numbers. It was a different car, more than fifty miles from where he'd seen the first license plate, but it was the same ZEN 666. It's another reminder that life is far more mysterious than we can imagine, and that the ultimate riddle, synchronicity, defies definition.

For Rob, the message of the first sighting was to adopt a zen-like attitude during a major transition in his life, urging him to go with the flow, to offer no resistance. If he could do this, then the trickster synchronicity seemed to promise he would emerge on the other side with greater wisdom. The second sighting confirmed he had succeeded.

UNDERSTANDING YOUR TRICKSTER

Trickster synchronicities can often be baffling, so you may have to do a bit of research to figure out what yours means. The obvious place to begin is Google.

When you Google "the trickster," more than four million sites come up. You'll find sites on the trickster in Native American mythology, the trickster and the paranormal, the trickster in movies and books, the trickster throughout history, the trickster in mythology. Click on one and start reading. Follow links to other sites.

In your research, you'll run across the classic trickster synchronicities, including the plum pudding story. Some will make you laugh out loud, others will mystify you. Maybe you're one of those people for whom a trickster synchronicity repeats over time.

In Bermuda in 1975, for example, a man riding a moped was struck and killed by a taxi driver. Exactly a year later, the man's brother was killed in the same way. That in itself qualifies as a synchronicity. But it gets even more puzzling. Both deaths happened on the same street, on the same moped, caused by the same taxi driver, who was carrying the same passenger. Four people were involved: the two brothers, the taxi driver, and the passenger. What was it in each of these individuals that invited a repeat of this situation and event? Was there supposed to be a lesson in this? The orchestration of these events has staggering implications about just how precise David Bohm's enfolded order may be.

If you experience this sort of serial trickster synchronicity, you may want to figure out why you continue to attract a particular experience. Look for metaphors, make associations, request a dream that will shed light on the issue. Talk to other people about your trickster. Create a Facebook page, blog, or discussion group about it. Your goal is to figure out the message. If you let other people in on your trickster stories, they might come up with possible meanings that never would occur to you.

Trickster Guises

The guises the trickster wears seem tailored to our individual needs and intentions. Depending on your situation and circumstances, the trickster warns, confirms, offers hope, pokes fun, and sometimes drives home the message about the interconnectedness of life. He can also bring your life full circle. But always, the trickster reminds you to laugh—at yourself and at the existential absurdities surrounding you.

Mike Clelland of Idaho discovered the trickster not only urges you to laugh, but the punch line to his synchronistic jokes can turn up in the most unlikely places. Mike spends a lot of time outdoors and is always looking for a sunblock that doesn't irritate his sensitive skin. A coworker suggested he try Neutrogena SPF-45. Mike went to the local health food store and the drug store looking for a bottle of it, but neither store carried the product. He hoped the giant supermarket in the strip mall might stock it, but he couldn't force himself to drive in that direction. "The creepiness of the grim strip mall just seemed to repel me."

Instead, he drove home. En route, he noticed large bags of trash set along the roadside for the annual spring trash clean up. Each year an organized group of volunteers in his area collects trash along the highway after the snow melts; because he lives on the highway, Mike often helps out. When he got home, he grabbed a few plastic trash bags and walked along the roadside picking up trash. He figured he would collect trash as far as the stop sign on the next corner, about a half a mile away.

"When I got to that stop sign, I found a full bottle of Neutrogena SPF-45. It was waiting for me—quite literally—at a sign post."

The bottle of sunblock turned out to be unusable, so the trickster got the last laugh. But the message was clear. By following the cues—not driving to the strip mall, surrendering to an impulse to participate in the highway cleanup—Mike received confirmation about the product and had a good laugh.

Trickster synchronicities are sometimes camouflaged in word puns. Movie producer Rob McKenzie was driving home from work one day when Peter Gabriel's song "Solsbury Hill" came on the radio. "When the song hit the 'My heart goin' boom-boom-boom' section of the chorus, I happened to look up at the sign of the street I was passing, which I'd never noticed before. It was Ann Gina Boulevard."

Angina, of course, is a heart condition that results in chest pain and an irregular heartbeat. The trickster was definitely poking fun at McKenzie. But there could also be a darker message in this synchronicity: McKenzie should get his heart checked.

Trickster synchronicities sometimes have a dark side and frequently, it's a warning. Sometimes the warnings are embedded in other experiences and situations—you have to be attentive to details to notice them.

Celeste Maia of Portugal related a story about a friend from Mozambique who was driving one day when a car cut in front of him. He noticed the number 19 repeated on the license plate. Later that day he encountered a friend who told him it was his son's nineteenth birthday. In various ways, the number 19 kept surfacing during the course of the day. The following day, Maia's friend had to travel by plane. Only seats 19A and 27 F were free. He chose 19A. During the flight a fire broke out. The plane had to make an emergency landing and nearly everyone onboard died except those sitting in aisle 19.

If the man hadn't been attentive enough to notice that first 19 on the license plate, he might have chosen seat 27F and died in the fire.

During your exploration of the world of synchronicity, the trickster may become your frequent companion. He's so adept at camouflage and surprise that it's easy to think you're experiencing one kind of synchronicity, only to discover the trickster grinning at you from the other side. One morning we were seated at an outdoor table at a neighborhood coffee shop discussing the outline for this book, when an elderly man approached us. He handed us a card that explained he was deaf and selling key chains. We bought one and, on the back of the card, found illustrations for sign language.

On the way home, following the cue from the deaf man, we talked about synchronicity as a language of signs. We passed the local high school, where the digital sign at the entrance advertised a class in sign language. We spotted a sign about sign language as we were talking about the language of signs, adding another layer to the synchronicity. At first, we interpreted it as confirmation about our approach to the book. But confirmation was just camouflage. Clearly the trickster was giving us a sign, seizing our attention, and driving home the point that first and foremost, writing the book should be fun.

When the trickster is being really mischievous, he may bring you face to face with a facet of your past that makes you uncomfortable. The odds involved in this kind of synchronicity are usually high, and your incredulity makes it impossible to ignore the fact that something important is happening.

Trish's dad, Tony, a retired accountant, was in his late eighties when he moved into an assisted living facility in Georgia, where Trish's sister was director of nursing. His wife of more than fifty years had died several years earlier—Parkinson's had stolen much of his mobility, and it was a lonely, isolated time for him. Several weeks after taking up residency, a woman in her eighties moved in across the hall. She turned out to be a former school classmate he'd known more than seventy years ago, when they both lived in a small town in Illinois.

Trish marveled at the synchronicity, but Tony wasn't amused. "The universe has a twisted sense of humor," he said. "I don't like her any more now than I did back then."

The message? Perhaps it's best expressed in the words of David Bohm: "Deep down, the consciousness of mankind is one." It was something Tony desperately needed to learn in this phase of his life.

The Trickster as Ally

Sometimes the trickster can improve the odds when your back is to the wall. That's the message of the following incident dating back to the early seventeenth century in the Scottish Highlands. For decades, the MacGregors and the Campbells had battled each other in disputes, usually involving land. In 1603, encouraged by the Campbells, King James VI issued an edict banning the use of the name MacGregor. The proscription on the name lasted until 1774.

In the early years of the proscription, MacGregors were hunted as criminals by the Campbells, and one of the most notorious of the outlaws was Callum MacGregor, grandfather of the famed Rob Roy.

In one of his numerous escapades, told by Forbes Mac-Gregor in *Clan Gregor*, Callum was hiding on an islet in Loch Katrine, and the Campbell men were camped on the woody shore, close enough for their voices to carry over the water. Callum had taken the precaution of sinking all the boats except the one he had used to reach the islet. Knowing the islet was barren, the Campbells thought they would starve Callum into surrender. As night fell, one of the band, a soutar, or cobbler by trade, lit a fire to prepare a meal. Callum took aim at the smoke, shouted a curse: "Thugad thall a chrom thruaill sloightear!" and fired. The bullet struck the cobbler in the forehead killing him. Loosely, the Gaelic translation means: "Get lost you slimy crook."

But, in Gaelic, the word for crook has a second meaning: cobbler. The Campbells had heard the shout but misinterpreted the meaning when the cobbler dropped dead. They quickly agreed that Callum had second sight and might pick them off one by one. After they fled in fear, Callum rowed to shore, escaped, and lived to enjoy a peaceful old age in Glengyle.

The Shadow Trickster

The Shadow, an archetype that focuses on the dark side of our personalities, pushes us to repeat whatever we're trying to avoid. For example, imagine there's someone you really dislike and don't want to see, but you keep running into that person repeatedly, in unlikely places and situations. Your resistance seems to attract him. It's awkward, annoying, maybe embarrassing, and you can't figure out what's going on. "When the shadow steals away one's purpose and turns it to his own amusement, he brings the hidden shadow out into the daylight," wrote Combs and Holland in *Synchronicity: Science, Myth, and the Trickster.*

When actors play the role of dark characters, they essentially live that reality, even if only for a short time. The stage is set for them to attract synchronicity through the shadow trickster, sometimes with tragic results. Take the case of Brandon Lee, who died while filming a scene in his last movie, *The Crow.*

In the scene in which Brandon was killed, his character, Eric Draven, found his girlfriend being raped by thugs who subsequently killed them both. Funboy, one of the film's villains, fired a gun at Brandon's character as he walked into his apartment carrying groceries. The gun was loaded with blanks, but a dummy cartridge had lodged in the barrel and the detonation of a blank was enough to propel it through the barrel. Fired from point-blank range, it penetrated Brandon's body, killing him.

Brandon's father, Bruce Lee, had died under similar mysterious circumstances during the filming of a movie, ironically named *Game of Death*, in 1978. Bruce Lee played a character who was shot to death, then returns from the dead to exact revenge. Adding to the irony, Brandon also died playing a character who is killed, then subsequently returns from the dead. Bruce Lee died at age thirty-two, Brandon at twenty-eight. Both deaths were ruled accidental but were considered highly suspicious.

Astonishingly, while working on this chapter in mid-2009, we were greeted by a front-page headline that screamed: "Star of 'Kung Fu,' 'Kill Bill' lived by the sword on the set." The headline echoed the refrain of the shadow trickster, and this time involved actor David Carradine.

In the early 1970s, Carradine played an enigmatic monk named Kwai Chang Caine, a martial arts expert who often ended each episode by beating the bad guys to a pulp. In 2004, he was cast as the head of a family of assassins and an expert swordsman in Quentin Tarantino's *Kill Bill* movies. At first, the news reports said Carradine hung himself in a luxury hotel room in Bangkok, where he was filming a new movie. But several news sources later reported he may have killed himself accidentally, after a dangerous sex act went wrong.

The shadow trickster was also at play in the death of actor Heath Ledger. At age twenty-eight, he was already a legend and an Oscar nominee for his role in *Brokeback Mountain*. He had just completed filming *The Dark Knight*, a Batman movie in which he played The Joker as it had never been played before.

The movie became only the second film in history to earn more than $500 million at the North American box office, and only the fourth film to earn more than $1 billion worldwide. Ledger won an Oscar for his performance. Unfortunately, Ledger died of an accidental overdose of prescription medications six months before the release of the film. Another dark character, another death. Ironically, Ledger was playing the role of the shadow trickster himself.

What are we to make of such synchronicities with negative impacts? One rule that dominates synchronicity is *like attracts like*. Even though the three men were merely acting dark roles, they experienced what it was like to live a life of violence and death. They were so involved in their roles they attracted the real-life experiences that led to their deaths. As Frank Joseph noted in *Synchronicity & You*, "Synchronicity, like death itself, has no respect for people."

British actor Joey Jeetun found that out when he barely escaped death during the terrorist attack in Mumbai, India, in November of 2008. He was in a restaurant in the financial district when the attacks started. Jeetun, who is most famous for playing the role of a terrorist bomber, recalled in the *London Times*, "I was covered in other people's blood. They thought I was dead."

Such synchronicities are sometimes labeled curses. In fact, the deaths of Bruce and Brandon Lee have been called the Curse of the Dragon because both men were born under that Chinese astrological symbol. But clearly it wasn't the shadow of their birth dates that caused their tragic deaths. It was their careers, synchronistically notable for filmed acts of violence. Ultimately, what we think is what we create.

Multiple Tricksters

Repetitive synchronicities were of great interest to Austrian biologist Paul Kammerer. He used to sit for hours in public areas, studying the people around him and taking note of how many carried umbrellas, for example, or wore certain types of hats. He studied repeated occurrences of numbers, names, places, dreams, letters, and disasters. Kammerer approached his research like the biologist he was, dissecting and eventually categorizing these synchronicities into first, second, third, and high-order series. He believed the phenomenon was an objective but undiscovered principle of nature and called it "the law of seriality." His research influenced Jung's early thoughts on synchronicity.

Kammerer would really get a kick out of what happened to Tony Vigorito, author of *Nine Kinds of Naked*, and would probably rate it as a high-order synchronicity. It was so baffling that at the time Tony couldn't fathom what was happening. It began as an accidental gathering of friends at his house in November 2004; everyone had stopped by uninvited. Someone brought a bottle of wine, another guest arrived with a guitar. Soon another guitar and a harmonica came out. Snacks appeared. Everyone sat around the fireplace on an old Oriental rug, the burning logs crackling as they ate, drank, talked, laughed, and played a few tunes.

At one point, a visual artist pulled a book entitled *Blue Dog Man* out of her bag. "It was the collected artwork of George Rodrigue, whose signature motif is the inclusion of a blue dog in all of his pieces, a terribly cute terrier/spaniel with eyes yearning for love and approval, apparently inspired by his deceased dog, Tiffany. The Blue Dog book was passed around and soon all of us were taking turns attempting to emulate Tiffany's sad and hopeful eyes."

Later in the evening, Tony checked his e-mail. The subject line of a message sent a couple hours earlier caught his attention. Eyes of a Blue Dog. Intrigued, he opened it and read comments from someone who had read something he'd written online. Surprisingly, there was no explanation of the subject line. He scrolled down and discovered the sender's name was Tiffany, the same as Rodrigue's dog.

Tony's credulity stretched to the breaking point. He called to his friends, who clustered around the computer and saw the subject line and the writer's name at the end of the e-mail. They were impressed, baffled, even astonished. Then someone noticed the signature line of Tiffany's e-mail, which sounded like a summary of the evening.

"Good atmosphere, good friends, good conversation, good wine, good books, and the space between."

Tony responded to Tiffany, asking for an explanation and offering a brief version of events that evening. The next day he found out she'd never heard of George Rodrigue or his dog Tiffany, but she had recently read the short story, *Eyes of a Blue Dog*, by Gabriel Garcia Marquez. She also wrote that she had only learned of the concept of synchronicity a month before in one of her psychology courses. The day before writing Tony, she'd arrived at her parents' house to find the word SYNCHRONIC-ITY written in caps across the Dry Erase Board in her parents' kitchen. Her father, it seems, had heard about synchronicity on a radio show and wanted to remind himself to read more about it.

Tony took his notebook computer to his favorite coffee-house and wrote the story of the previous evening's events, and the follow up. "As I sat there writing . . . should it really surprise anyone that 'I Am the Walrus' came on the stereo?"

WORKING WITH THE TRICKSTER ELEMENT

As you become more aware of synchronicities, they'll occur more frequently, especially if you take time to record them. Synchronicities are sometimes found in your immediate environment through the behavior of birds and other animals, weather patterns, a voice on the radio or TV. Note which synchronicities are tricksters, those that jolt you into a higher awareness of the interconnection between the mundane and the extraordinary.

You can attempt to generate synchronicities and even specific types, such as trickster synchronicities. Tell yourself you're going to experience synchronicity, perhaps one of the trickster variety—but be sure to add that the experience will not harm you or anyone else. Sometimes such synchronicities will be as obvious as a splash of cold water in the face. Other times, they can be so subtle you don't recognize them immediately.

For instance, when we started the rewrites on this chapter, we were hoping to find another strong example of a trickster synchronicity. Within moments, a friend sent us a story about a coyote that survived impossible odds when it was struck by a car traveling at seventy-five miles an hour and became lodged behind the grill in front of the engine. In esoteric traditions, the coyote is known as the trickster.

Stay alert for "coincidental" encounters that might otherwise slip by you unnoticed. Sometimes we focus on the drama of events and miss the obvious synchronicity. You may look back at the end of the day at everything significant that occurred and suddenly discover synchronicity sneaked up on you, like a trickster.

Secret 7

THE GLOBAL

When synchronicities manifest themselves through global events, the universe seems to be addressing us as a collective.

"You cannot begin to understand the nature of mass events of any kind unless you consider the even greater framework in which they have their existence."

—JANE ROBERTS, *THE INDIVIDUAL AND THE NATURE OF MASS EVENTS*

Whether you live in Alabama or Albania, in Prague or Peoria, in Santiago or San Francisco, the individual who occupies the U.S. White House has an enormous bearing on the quality of your life. Given the controversial nature of George Bush's two terms in office, it was stunning to witness the way the universe spoke through synchronicity as Bush's second term came to an end.

On January 15, 2009 at 8:00 P.M., the president gave his final speech to the nation. In a presidency defined by the repercussions of planes slamming into the World Trade Center, it was intriguing that just five hours earlier, U.S. Airways flight 1549 crashed into the Hudson River, a short distance from the tragic site of 9/11. Yet, the landing was near perfect, and all 155 passengers survived.

The first rescue boat to reach the scene was named after Thomas Jefferson, the principal author of the Declaration of Independence, a staunch supporter of the separation between church and state, a man consistently ranked as one of our best presidents. After eight years of flagrant abuse of power, a disastrous war of choice, torture, rendition flights, and the erosion of civil rights, it was as if the "miracle on the Hudson" was the universe assuring us that we would come through it all intact. It's no small irony that five days later, the day after Martin Luther King Day, the first African-American U.S. president was sworn into office.

Through mass events and the synchronicities so often associated with them, the universe speaks to us as a collective—as a people, a community, a nation, as citizens of the same planet. These types of synchronicities certainly illustrate connections to a deeper layer of existence, similar to what quantum physicists speak of when they refer to everything in the universe being intimately connected. As Michael Talbot put it in *The Holographic Universe*, "Our brains mathematically construct objective reality by interpreting frequencies that are ultimately projections from a deeper order of existence that is beyond space and time—the brain is a hologram enfolded in a holographic universe."

Synchronicities in the News

In this era of 24/7 news coverage, most of us have heard or read a national story that we recognized as a meaningful coincidence. On occasion, the cable news broadcasters comment on them. At the end of the funeral for NBC broadcaster Tim Russert, "Somewhere Over the Rainbow" played, and as family and friends left the church, a double rainbow burst across the sky. Fellow broadcaster Keith Olbermann noted the synchronicity on his program the next evening, though he didn't use the term.

As part of the memorial service for the seven astronauts who died in the 1986 Challenger disaster, wreaths were dropped from a helicopter off the Florida coast. A pod of dolphins unexpectedly surfaced near the wreaths. The film of the event was shown repeatedly on news broadcasts. NASA scientists studied it and counted the dolphins; even though only five were visible, scientists speculated there were at least two more in the pod— one for each astronaut.

The dolphins' spontaneous appearance at the dramatic ceremony was inspiring and reassuring, symbolic of a larger picture. Greek and Mediterranean legends treat the dolphin as a creature of good fortune and intelligence, a talisman for voyages not only on the sea but also into the afterlife.

In the late 1990s, five-year-old Elian Gonzalez fled Cuba with his mother and ten other people on a small craft. When the craft sank, everyone onboard drowned except Elian, who was found on Thanksgiving Day 1999, floating off the coast of Florida. A fierce custody battle ensued between Elian's father in Cuba and his relatives in Miami. Because the boy was supposedly saved by dolphins that kept him afloat after the other passengers drowned, a kind of religious movement grew up around him.

Take a few moments to think about mass events—disasters, invasions, large-scale demonstrations, deaths of public figures— and try to remember any synchronicities related to them. Maybe you had a dream or premonition about such an event. Maybe you had a connection with someone involved in the event, or a connection with the location. Chances are that the events, which captured your attention, carried some personal significance.

9/11

Millions of people around the world watched the World Trade Center disaster unfold on television as it was happening. For weeks afterward, it dominated worldwide media coverage. In the aftermath of the attack, thousands of personal synchronicities were recorded about the events. If you Google "9/11 synchronicities," tens of thousands of sites come up, many of them stories of survival that illustrate how personal synchronicities are often enfolded within mass events.

Three weeks before the World Trade Center disaster, we were visiting friends in Cassadaga, Florida, a spiritualist community.

Medium Art Burley was giving Rob a reading focused on his career when Burley suddenly caught his breath and looked up. "I see two huge explosions coming, from above, like huge bombs. It's coming very soon. It's going to be enormous and will change everything." Apparently still thinking that he was talking about Rob's career, he added, "It could be a movie. It's big." Of course, it wasn't a movie, it was real, and the bombs weren't a metaphor for a career change. They were two commercial jets turned into bombs as they struck their targets.

British biologist and author Rupert Sheldrake sensed that psychic experiences related to 9/11 would abound. He placed a newspaper ad in the *Village Voice* and posters in Union Square in New York City, seeking dreams and premonitions related to the tragedy. He received fifty-seven responses; thirty-eight involved precognitive dreams, fifteen were related to premonitions. About a third of the dreams occurred the night before the disaster and another third during the preceding five to six days.

Sheldrake felt the people who responded represented a fraction of those who probably experienced related premonitions. Several respondents dreamed of buildings collapsing, explosions in New York, airplanes crashing into buildings, or people fleeing in panic. The responses that most impressed Sheldrake came from people who told others about their dreams before the terrorist attack and premonitions from people who rarely experience such a sense of foreboding.

Mike Chirni, a forensic scientist who lives in New York City, dreamed of flying low over buildings he recognized in Manhattan. He and others on the plane were upset. He felt an overwhelming sense of dread, then a tremendous impact, and woke up.

Amanda Bernsohn, who worked three blocks from the World Trade Center, didn't know why she couldn't stop crying the night of September 10. When she finally fell asleep, she dreamed not of the World Trade Center, but of Nazis taking over New York. She overslept for the first time since she'd started her job eight months earlier and was awakened by a call from a friend shortly after the first plane struck the North Tower.

Not surprisingly, an event like 9/11 reverberated through time. Back in the early 1990s, Vicki DeLaurentis lived in the suburbs of Philadelphia and attended a day-long spiritual retreat with past-life regressionist Carol Bowman. During a guided meditation into the future, Vicki saw the Twin Towers on fire and crumbling to the ground. She had no idea when this would happen, but her spirit guide assured her she wouldn't be there when it did. For years, she tried to figure out the timing and asked every psychic she knew, but none of them had any inkling of anything like this.

In 1997, she and her husband moved to Long Island, and she really began to worry about what she'd seen in Carol's workshop. Her husband was employed in the oil business and his traders worked in the World Trade Center. Still, her guide reassured her she would be fine.

Fast forward to 2001. Vicki's husband had a meeting in the WTC, scheduled for September 11. He and Vicki decided to have dinner that evening at Windows on the World, the restaurant atop the World Trade Center. Vicki, who has a fear of heights, felt uneasy about it. However, a week before 9/11, her husband's meeting was postponed until the 12th. "If the original meeting hadn't been changed, my husband would have been there."

HEALING ENERGY EXERCISE

When a major event occurs, especially a disaster, it's natural to feel frightened and confused. Our immediate reaction is a concern for our lives and the lives of our loved ones. Whether it's a natural event, such as a hurricane, or a manmade one, we eventually start to wonder why it happened and what it will mean to us in the future. Here's an exercise that can lead you toward inner awareness.

Sit comfortably, take several deep breaths, then gradually slow your breath. Feel your body relaxing, feel your mind relaxing. Forget your to-do list. Tell yourself that you're going to reach a place of inner healing; you're going to attract the energy you need to heal yourself and to spread that healing to others.

Visualize an energetic essence surrounding your body. See it as a glowing golden light. See it radiating around you, then focus the golden light around your heart. See it filling your body, healing, cleansing, rejuvenating, pulling positive energy into your life. Try to stay focused on this energy for at least five minutes. When your mind starts to wander, bring it back to the golden light.

Before you come out of your meditation, imagine again that you'll be taking the healing energy with you. See a layer of violet light surrounding the golden light, allowing you to move the healing energy out into the world. Whenever you interact positively with others, see the healing energy spreading. Imagine it moving from person to person, spreading around the world, healing old wounds, physical, mental, and spiritual ones.

MOVIE "PREVIEWS" OF 9/11

A website called Conspiracy Archive features an intriguing collection of 9/11 references that appeared in films long before September 11. For instance, in the 1996 film *Independence Day,* one scene depicts the president and his family being evacuated in Air Force One. Actor Jeff Goldblum opens his laptop to watch the countdown and the camera cuts to a close-up of the clock: 9:11:01.

The Peacemaker, a 1997 film starring George Clooney and Nicole Kidman, includes a scene at JFK Airport, where the stars are pursuing a Yugoslavian terrorist. As Clooney steps off an escalator, two desks are visible behind him, numbered 9 and 11.

In *Enemy of the State,* a 1998 film, a computer search by Gene Hackman and Will Smith turns up personal data on a corrupt politician played by Jon Voight in the film. His birth date is 9/11/40. In the opening scenes of the 2000 film *Traffic,* a drug van is seized and pulled over. When the cargo is revealed, every carton is stamped 911.

Although the website is obviously skewed toward the conspiracy angle, we see these movie references as synchronicities, specifically precognition. The collective shock of 9/11 reverberated through space and time, as the research of the Global Consciousness Project has shown.

The Global Consciousness Project

The dramatic impact of the WTC disaster became a natural target for a scientific study aimed at monitoring what author Dean Radin called the "global mind." The Global Consciousness Project, based at Princeton University and cosponsored by the Institute of Noetic Sciences, is an Internet-based experiment started by Princeton's Dr. Roger Nelson. Since 1998, it has monitored the movements of this global mind. Radin, writing in the May 2003 issue of *IONSNoetic Sciences Review*, described the project as "an ocean of individual minds . . . that explores the mind-matter relationship" by using a random number generator (RNG).

The network consists of sixty-five sites worldwide that generate random numbers. Once per minute, these numbers are downloaded and analyzed to find out how consistent they are. As explained at the Global Consciousness Project Dot website (*www.gcpdot.com*), "Our purpose is to examine subtle correlations that may reflect the presence and activity of consciousness in the world. We predict structure in what should be random data, associated with major global events." In everyday terms, repeatedly flipping a coin should result in an equal number of heads and tails. But *during* events of high global interest, according to the theory of global consciousness, the focused attention and emotional outpouring results in a notable difference in the percentage of heads versus tails.

Radin noted that the events of 9/11 provided a tragic but edifying test for the project, due to the nature of the events, the heightened emotions, and the massive media coverage. On 9/11, thirty-seven of the random-number generators were active. The fluctuations in the bell curve analysis indicated that anomalies began two hours before the first plane hit the WTC, odds of 20 to 1, Radin noted. The results that day were the fifteenth largest out of nearly 1,400 days. "That means that on that fateful day, the GCP's 'bells' collectively rang out around the world with an unusually pure tone."

What, exactly, is this global mind? Nelson, the project's innovator, describes the global mind as the combined consciousness of every person on the planet. "Consciousness has a creative, productive, generative role in the world such that what we wish for is more likely to be than if we hadn't wished for it," he wrote on GCP's website. "What we envision together will manifest in the world in a subtle way."

In 2003, Dean Radin noted that after he and his colleagues published their findings about 9/11 in the physics journal *Foundations of Physics Letters*, some scientists were skeptical. In the course of explaining how he explored the analysis of the RNG, he said, "If the Global Consciousness Project is detecting genuine, large-scale mind-matter interactions, then it raised the possibility that some coincidences may be more than just dumb luck." Then he related two astonishing synchronicities related to the 2002 memorial events for 9/11.

On the evening of September 11, 2002, the New York Lottery drew the sequence 9-1-1. Radin said the chance probability of selecting any given three-number sequence is 1 in 1,000. A bit of investigation revealed that in the previous 5,000 drawings of this lottery, the 9-1-1 sequence had come up five times. "However, is it a coincidence that this number appeared on this date, in this city, and not in any of the other state lotteries? Given the massive attention placed on the sequence 9-1-1 on that day and in that city, it does make one wonder."

The next synchronicity occurred at ground zero in Manhattan, also on September 11, 2002. The weather that day was calm, the sky was blue and clear, no storms were predicted. Yet, as reported by the *Milwaukee Journal Sentinel*, shortly before the commemoration ceremony was to begin the winds whipped up and the air filled with dust, just as it had a year earlier as the towers fell.

A month later, *Windsurfer* magazine published an article written by a windsurfer who was there. "After witnessing the strong wind that 'came out of nowhere,' the windsurfer checked the wind records for September 11 and for the previous few days," Radin wrote in *IONS Noetic Science Review*. "The results were striking: For a week before September 11, 2002, the winds near New York City were calm, averaging about five miles an hour. On September 11, around 9 A.M., the winds in the bay near Long Island suddenly shot up over 45 miles an hour."

Radin was impressed enough by this story to check with the National Weather Service station in Central Park and also at Dulles Airport near Washington, D.C. And yes, both locations experienced changes in barometric pressure and wind speed, starting around 9:00 A.M. Radin wrote, "This ongoing experiment suggests that as mass mind moves, so does matter."

The theory upon which the Global Consciousness Project is founded has roots that reach back to ancient times. In the fourth century B.C., Greek philosopher Heraclitus saw all things as interrelated or following "cosmic reason." He believed events were not isolated happenings, but had repercussions across the entire fabric of existence, that all things were linked by a web of organization created by Logos.

Hippocrates, born twenty years after Heraclitus died, expressed similar thoughts. "There is one common flow, a common breathing. Everything is in sympathy. The whole organism and each one of its parts are working together for the same purpose. The great principle extends to the most extreme part, and from the extremest part returns again to the great principle."

The Roman scholar Agrippa referred to a Fifth Essence— something beyond earth, air, fire, and water—that held existence together. He also called it the World Soul, which penetrates all things and is a thing in itself. Agrippa's contemporary, Plotinus wrote, "Chance has no place in life, but only harmony and order reign therein."

In the Middle Ages, this idea was known as the *unus mundus*, one world, and referred to a collective knowledge that exists independently of us, yet is available to us. In this cosmology, the source of meaningful coincidence is separate from our conscious awareness and egos, but it's where the psyche and the external world touch.

It sounds a lot like F. David Peat's theory that synchronicity is a bridge between mind and external reality: In *Synchronicity: The Bridge Between Matter and Mind,* he wrote, "Synchronicities . . . open the floodgates of the deeper levels of consciousness and matter which, for a creative instant, sweep over the mind and heal the division between the internal and the external."

Sometimes, synchronicities associated with mass events blow open our awareness that the universe isn't what it appears to be. Author Daniel Pinchbeck, in *2012: The Return of Quetzalcoatl,* wrote how in September 2001 he finally got around to editing a friend's "poetic manifesto," a kind of diatribe against corporatism and globalization. His partner was in the bedroom, feeding their infant daughter, and he had the pages of the poet's manuscript spread out on a table in the living room when they suddenly heard something outside, which he described as "the roar of a low-flying airplane and then a loud metallic crunch." He and his partner opened the blinds and "saw a flaming crater in one of the World Trade towers." The title of his friend's manuscript was *World on Fire.*

Pinchbeck grew up with a materialist belief system that would've dismissed such a coincidence as the product of probability or random chance. According to the materialist way, the brain naturally seeks to find patterns. "As a by-product of our habitual pattern-seeking, we are neurologically programmed to seek deeper meanings in a world that is, at the most fundamental level, devoid of such things," Pinchbeck wrote. "Our belief that there are 'signs' hidden within the chaos of events is an age-old survival mechanism, an attempt to endow our lives with importance and avoid the existential fact of our insignificance."

He went on to update his perspective. "Although I didn't realize it at the time, deep currents of twentieth-century thought, in the disciplines of physics and psychoanalysis, suggest this materialist perspective is a flawed one."

Registering Premonitions

Forums for registering premonitions about disasters have existed in one form or another since the aftermath of the Aberfan mining disaster in 1966 when the Central Premonition Registry was created. In that incident, a coal mine collapsed in the Welsh village of Aberfan, causing an avalanche that killed 144 people, including 116 children. The disaster attracted worldwide attention.

A British psychologist named Dr. John Barker suspected that some residents in the nearby villages might have had premonitions of the dramatic event. He made inquiries and received seventy-six reports. Of those, he corroborated twenty-four.

One of the most accurate premonitions came from a forty-seven-year-old woman who dreamed of an old school building in a valley, a Welsh coal miner, and an avalanche of coal tumbling down a mountain slope. Near the bottom of the mountain was a frightened boy. She saw a rescue effort and knew the boy had been saved. The day before the disaster, she told the dream to six people at her church.

A year after the disaster, Dr. Barker established the British Premonitions Bureau. The following year Robert and Nancy Nelson founded a similar organization in New York, called the Central Premonitions Registry. The current registry is called Prophecies: Prediction and Premonition Registry and can be found online at *www.prophecies.us*. These organizations gathered reports of dreams that might foretell future events that could impact large numbers of people in order to warn them of upcoming disasters. However, most premonitions of disaster tend to occur a day or two before the event, making it difficult to act upon such reports.

The Personal Enfolded Within the Global

Although preventing tragedy through premonitions seems challenging, F. David Peat recounts a story in which a healer stopped a disaster. The story originated with Richard Wilhelm, a friend of Jung's who is best known for his 1950 translation of the *I Ching* into English.

The village had gone for weeks without rain, and the villagers called in a rainmaker. Instead of performing complicated rituals to bring on the rains, the man went straight to the hut that had been provided for him. He realized the village was suffering from discord, that it was out of step with nature. Once the rainmaker had composed himself, equilibrium was restored to the village and the rains fell. In a sense, the village was experiencing a collective spiritual crisis. The rainmaker served as the catalyst to its resolution.

In the same way, in the fourth century A.D., St. Augustine faced a spiritual crisis in his life. As he paced around the garden of Milan, he heard a child's voice from a nearby house mysteriously repeating the words, "*Tolle, lege, tolle, lege.*" Pick up and read, pick up and read.

Baffled, he finally opened a copy of St. Paul's epistles and read a response to his lifelong conflict—the passage even addressed its resolution. "The light of certainty flooded my heart and all dark shadows of doubt fled away," he later wrote in Book VIII of *The Confessions of St. Augustine*, said to be the first autobiography in Western literature. The child's voice, like the rainmaker in the Chinese village, helped when help was needed most. Both cases were clear examples of synchronicity.

A thousand years later, St. Augustine's writings led to the birth of the Renaissance through the visions of Petrarch. The Italian scholar and poet, born in 1304, is known as the father of humanism and was one of the first to label the Middle Ages as the Dark Ages. For years, he thought about climbing Mont Ventoux to get a panoramic view of the region. Mountain climbing was a rarity back then, especially for the purpose of obtaining a better view. In April 1336, however, Petrarch and his brother began the ascent that scholars would later regard as the event that symbolized the onset of the Renaissance.

When he reached the summit, with clouds drifting below his feet, the wind in his face, Petrarch was astonished by the view of French Provence, the Alps, the Mediterranean. In his exhilarated state, he opened his copy of *The Confessions of St. Augustine*. Turning at random to book X, he read: "And men go abroad to admire the heights of mountains, the mighty billows of the sea, the broad tide of rivers, the compass of the ocean, and the circuit of the stars, and pass themselves by . . . ."

Petrarch marveled at what he read, recognizing the coincidence as part of a larger pattern, a transformative moment. He later wrote in a letter that it couldn't have been an accident that he had happened upon these very words. "What I had there read I believed to be addressed to me and to no other, remembering that St. Augustine had once suspected the same thing in his own case."

The experiences of St. Augustine and Petrarch became not only pivotal turning points in their own journeys of awakening, but had a global impact as well. Likewise, Daniel Pinchbeck's experience blew open his awareness and shifted his intellectual orientation from a materialist perspective to a synchronistic one. It led him to think and write in the footsteps of Terence McKenna, Timothy Leary, and Aldous Huxley. The personal enfolded within the global.

JFK, Lincoln, and Obama

In the aftermath of the shocking assassination of John F. Kennedy in 1963, a list of astonishing similarities between Kennedy and Abraham Lincoln came to light. Although others have been added over the years, the strongest synchronicities were those noted shortly after JFK died.

- Kennedy was elected to Congress in 1946; Lincoln was elected to Congress in 1846.
- JFK was elected President in 1960; Lincoln was elected in 1860.
- Lincoln had a secretary named Kennedy.
- Kennedy was shot in a car named Lincoln.
- Lincoln was shot in a theater named Ford; Kennedy was shot in a car made by Ford.
- Both men were shot in the back of the head on a Friday, while their wives sat next to them.

- Lincoln gave blacks freedom and legalized equality; Kennedy enforced equality for blacks.
- Both men were succeeded by men named Johnson.
- Lincoln's Vice President Andrew Johnson was born in 1808; Kennedy's Vice President Lyndon Johnson was born in 1908.
- Lincoln was shot in a theater and his assassin ran to a warehouse; JFK was shot from a warehouse and his alleged assassin ran to a theater.
- Lincoln's assassin had a three-worded name, John Wilkes Booth; Kennedy's alleged assassin had a three-worded name, Lee Harvey Oswald.
- John Wilkes Booth was born in 1839; Lee Harvey Oswald was born in 1939.
- Kennedy's father had been the ambassador to England at the Court of St James; Lincoln's son became the ambassador to England at the Court of St James.
- Lincoln had two sons, Robert and Edward. Edward died young, Robert lived on. Kennedy had two brothers, Robert and Edward. Robert died young, Edward lived on.

The parallels between these two men are dramatic. To dismiss them as mere oddities is not only shortsighted, but reveals an unwillingness to glimpse a deeper reality hidden from the everyday world. When we allow ourselves to look, to *really* look, our rational minds reel. Just as the world was riveted to television in the aftermath of 9/11, so were millions riveted in the aftermath of Kennedy's assassination. Mass events affect mass consciousness and create an environment fertile for synchronicity.

When Barack Obama became the forty-fourth president of the United States, many noted the synchronicities between him and Lincoln. Both men were lawyers who began their political careers in the Illinois state legislature, serving in the same district. Both served a single term in Congress before becoming president. Both brought young children to the White House. They were both propelled into the national spotlight by powerful speeches. Neither man served in the military. Lincoln freed the slaves and Obama is the first African-American president of the United States.

The life stories of Lincoln and Obama reveal fascinating parallels, just as the death stories of Lincoln and Kennedy were synchronistically connected.

NEDA: THE DIVINE CALLING

After the June 2009 presidential election in Iran, massive demonstrations erupted as Iranians protested the results. It looked as though the election was rigged and the populous was rebelling against the status quo. Any uprising that involves masses of people, intense emotions, and worldwide media coverage is likely to involve synchronicity. While watching the news the next day, we found a dramatic instance of it.

A beautiful young woman's death on the street during a demonstration was highlighted and quickly became a symbol of the movement. The graphic video was shown on cable news over and over and spread across the Internet.

The synchronicity was her name: Neda in Farsi means The Divine Calling. Her death was seen as a sacrifice to a greater cause.

Measuring the Line Between Mind and Matter

On October 3, 1995, an estimated half-billion people watched or listened to the live broadcast of the verdict in the O. J. Simpson murder case. It was the most publicized murder case ever. Reuters reported that the viewing audience for this event surpassed three of the five Super Bowl telecasts between 1991 and 1995.

Dean Radin, Roger Nelson, and a colleague at the University of Amsterdam were ready for the event with five random number generators (RNGs). They were looking for unusual correlations in what should be random data that would indicate heightened activity in the global consciousness.

"We expected that the unusual degree of mass attention focused on this evening would cause the combined output of five independent RNGs simultaneously to show unexpected order when the verdict was announced," Radin wrote in *IONS Noetic Sciences Review* in the summer of 1998.

And that's exactly what happened. The global mind—the *unus mundus*—was so focused on the O. J. verdict that it impacted the random number generators in a measurable way. Around 9:00 A.M. Pacific time on October 3, 1995, when the TV coverage about the impending verdict began, "an unexpected degree of order appeared in all the RNGs," Radin reported.

A graph that accompanied the article showed a spike during the hour when coverage began. It resembled the sort of lines you might see on a seismograph as a quake reaches its greatest intensity. A second, greater spike culminated as the verdict was announced.

Radin said this experiment, and others like it, illustrate that the common link between mind and matter is order. It echoes Bohm's implicate order, and smacks of synchronicity.

Move ahead thirteen years. On October 3, 2008, thirteen years to the day after O. J. Simpson was acquitted of double homicide, he was convicted of kidnapping, armed robbery, and ten other charges. He and five men had stormed a room in a hotel casino, where they seized plaques, photos, and game balls. The O. J. story had come full circle.

THINKING GLOBALLY

We share the planet with nearly seven billion people, so it behooves us to pay attention to what's going on in the larger world and to look for synchronicities related to global events that may hold vital clues about future trends. Keep a list of them and be as detailed as possible. What do the deeper messages tell you about the future? About the landscape of global politics, war, and peace? About global warming? About the role of the individual within society? How does all of this relate to you?

Consider arranging your file of global synchronicities by categories. Here are some suggestions:

- Politics
- International affairs
- Famous people
- Finances/economy
- Spirituality and religion
- National mood
- Discoveries/inventions
- Disasters and war
- Triumphs

In which category do you notice the most synchronicities? What kinds of synchronicities do you find? Metaphorical? Precognitive? Literal?

Connie Cannon, a numerologist, experiences frequent synchronicities in precognitive dreams that are related to famous people. Connie is also physically sensitive to pending earthquakes. Several days before a cluster of quakes, or quakes rated 5.0 or above, she experiences a variety of symptoms including extreme vertigo, nausea, and soaring blood pressure. It took her years to make the correlation between earthquakes and her symptoms, but now she can sometimes pinpoint the areas where quakes will occur based on the types of symptoms she experiences.

Another friend of ours will occasionally see newspaper headlines on the current edition that no one else sees— only to find those exact or similar headlines a day or two later. It happens spontaneously to her. With practice, and if you're inclined, you might develop this talent.

Sit down every morning and gaze at the front page of the newspaper. You might focus on a particular category of global events that interests you, or remain open to any remarkable developments.

Slow your breathing; shut your eyes. Press your thumb against your right nostril; breathe in through your left. Hold the air for a few seconds, then remove your thumb and exhale through the right nostril. Repeat, this time blocking your left nostril and inhaling through the right one. This type of breathing balances the hemispheres of your brain. Go back and forth a few times. With eyes closed, lay your hand on the newspaper.

Once you feel centered, take away your hand and stare "through" the newspaper. Allow your vision to "unfocus." If you prefer, you can keep your eyes closed. As you take a few more deep breaths, you might start to see headlines from the future. When images of headlines appear, jot them down.

Part Two
The Magic

PART TWO

The Magic

DIVINING
SYNCHRONICITY

"Divination is like a demonstration laboratory: it shows us how the elements of daily life are moved and shaped by the greater force of Primary Reality."

—DIANNE SKAFTE, *LISTENING TO THE ORACLE*

From the *I Ching* to astrology, from the tarot and runes to the patterns made by tea leaves, coffee grounds, or bones, synchronicity is the engine that drives all divination systems. Whatever the method and the means, divination is the most tangible way to engage synchronicity.

Divination has been practiced since the earliest stages of civilization and probably began before humans discovered fire. Among the ancient Babylonians, diviners read patterns in animal entrails, with a special emphasis on the liver, in smoke, oil on the surface of water, and through the behavior of animals, cats in particular. The Babylonians, like the Chinese, Egyptians, Greeks, Asians, and Persians, also used astrology.

The Druids favored crystal balls and read patterns in clouds and stars, knotted tree roots, and the calls of birds. Around 1,200 B.C., the Chinese used a divination system called *fuji*, which bears some resemblance to a Ouija board. The ancient Greeks had their Oracle at Delphi but also divined patterns in dreams, in the murmurs of springs, and by tossing small stones or pieces of wood, knucklebones, or dice.

"The history of divination has no starting point and no destination. It is woven so tightly into the spiritual life of humankind that we cannot imagine a time when some form of divining was not used," wrote Dianne Skafte in *Listening to the Oracle*.

The one thing all these systems had in common was the creation of meaningful patterns intrinsic to the moment. However, as Jung pointed out in his introduction to the Richard Wilhelm translation of the *I Ching*, any pattern is meaningful only if you're able to relate the interpretation to events in your life. When you do so, you're gaining guidance from the unconscious mind, which is linked to the underlying reality, the collective unconscious. In essence, the practice of divination is our most immediate contact with synchronicity.

The I Ching

The *I Ching* has been around for at least five thousand years, but was introduced to a larger Western audience in 1950 through the translation of Richard Wilhelm, a European who spent most of his life translating ancient Chinese texts. The divination system is based on sixty-four patterns known as hexagrams, which are derived by tossing three coins six times. Originally, bones were used and later, stalks of yarrow.

Hexagrams consist of six horizontal lines, either broken or unbroken. Using the coins, heads (*yang*) equals three points, tails (*yin*) equals two points. So two heads and a tail would equal an eight. Six and eight are broken lines; seven and nine are unbroken. Here's an example of a hexagram.

In addition, sixes and nines are "changing lines" that suggest the present situation is in flux. These lines lead you to a second hexagram, the evolution of your question. You consult a table in the back of the book to find the name and number of the hexagram(s) you've created, then look up the interpretation.

As Jung wrote in the introduction to the Wilhelm edition, whoever invented the *I Ching* believed that the hexagram "was the exponent of the moment in which it was cast."

In other words, when you toss the coins, the hexagram you receive is like a snapshot in time, making manifest the internal. In *The Invisible Landscape: Mind, Hallucinogens, and the I Ching*, authors and visionary scholars Terence and Dennis McKenna wrote that they believed the hexagrams of the *I Ching* were archetypes "that could shed light on one's fate if one properly consulted the oracle."

We asked the *I Ching* about the importance of synchronicity and received hexagram 15 "Modesty." In part, it reads: "It dispenses the blessings of heaven, the clouds and rain that gather round its summit, and thereafter shines forth radiant with heavenly light." That hexagram changed to number 45 "Gathering Together," which suggests: "In the time of gathering together we must arm promptly to ward off the unexpected. Human woes usually come as a result of unexpected events against which we are not forearmed. If we are prepared, they can be prevented."

In other words, these hexagrams seemed to say that synchronicities are blessings and that paying attention to these meaningful coincidences is a way of heeding warnings and gathering information to prepare for the future.

After Adele Aldridge separated from her husband, she wanted to get in touch with an old friend whom she'd heard had recently divorced. She didn't know how to reach him, but her desire was strong. In a dream she saw a winged horse flying across the sky. She didn't have any idea what it meant, but loved the imagery and felt it was a strong message of something extraordinary. She asked the *I Ching* for insight into the dream's meaning. The response was hexagram 22 "Grace" with the fourth line changing. The Wilhelm translation for this changing line is:

GRACE OR SIMPLICITY?
A white horse comes as if on wings.
He is not a robber,
He will woo at the right time."

"I had goose flesh when I read that. Not only did the *I Ching* reflect my dream with eerie accuracy, but the next day the person I wanted to see called me." The dream and the *I Ching* reading—and the subsequent connection—marked the beginning of life-changing events for her.

YOU AND THE *I CHING*
If you're not familiar with the *I Ching* and want to try it, head to your nearest bookstore and look for one of the many editions in the New Age section. Our favorite is the popular Richard Wilhelm/Cary F. Baynes edition. Other translations strive to make the lexicon of ancient Chinese life more comprehensible to Westerners. Take your translation into the café, order a coffee, get out three pennies, and think of a question. Then toss your coins and see what happens. Or, Google "I Ching free readings" to get an online taste of what it's all about.

Granted, the *I Ching* isn't for everyone. Some of the hexagrams that address the roles of women in ancient Chinese society are blatantly sexist by today's standards. References to the harvest and drought don't have much tangible relevance to twenty-first-century life unless you work in the agricultural industry. But if you set aside your Western bias and distill the essence of the hexagrams, you can glean much wisdom from this divination system. It's especially good for gaining insight into dreams and the dynamics of an evolving situation.

People who use this system regularly attest to its uncanny accuracy. It works best if you're accustomed to interpreting metaphors and making associations. Sometimes, following the advice of the *I Ching* can be an act of faith.

For instance, in *Synchronicity: Multiple Perspectives on Meaningful Coincidence*, Shantena Augusto Sabbadini tells a story about his *I Ching* mentor, Rudolph Ritsema, who spent fifty years studying the oracle, translating it, and using it. When he was admitted to a Swiss clinic with a brain hemorrhage, his physicians were concerned about his heart condition and thought he needed a pacemaker. Before making his decision about the insertion of the pacemaker, Ritsema, who was paralyzed on the left side from the brain hemorrhage, consulted the *I Ching*, then decided not to have the procedure. His doctors were dumbfounded. Ritsema was already in his 80s, and died a few years later at age 88, but he had faith in a system in which he believed.

"Synchronicity . . . deals with the non-repeatable, with the non-reproducible," wrote Sabbadini. "A synchronistic event—even an *I Ching* consultation—speaks to us through the specifics of a constellation of inner and outer circumstances that will never again recur in exactly the same pattern. . . . Synchronicity is a one-time phenomenon."

And as a one-time phenomenon, its advice is often eerily accurate.

Astrology

As a divination tool, astrology is as rich and complex as the *I Ching*. Instead of yarrow sticks or coins, astrology is based on the patterns and movements of the heavenly bodies at any given time. A natal chart or horoscope is a geometrical diagram of the heavens as seen from your birthplace at the moment you were born. The chart is determined by the date, time, and place of your birth and looks like a circle with twelve unequal sections. These sections are known as houses and depict different areas of your life: self, finances, siblings and neighbors, family, partners, and so on. Just as the *I Ching* coin toss is a snapshot in time, the moment you drew your first breath froze an instant in time. A birth chart, like a hexagram, forms a meaningful pattern, a blueprint of archetypal potential.

Many mainstream scientists and educators dismiss astrology as a superstition of the past and view astronomy as the science of celestial bodies. Yet, the father of modern astronomy, Galileo Galilei, was also an astrologer. He was attacked by the Church for his astrological predictions as well as his astronomical calculations and spent much of his life under house arrest.

In spite of efforts throughout the centuries to discredit astrology, it remains a vibrant means of analyzing personalities and relationships—and predicting the future. Some scientists, in fact, have been baffled by its accuracy.

In 1950, French statistician Michel Gauquelin set out to prove that the birth positions of the stars and planets exert no influence whatsoever on one's future development. He was dismayed when his own statistics proved him wrong, with five million-to-one odds against pure chance showing that great soldiers, military leaders, and warlords tended to have Mars ascending in their horoscopes.

Many types of astrology can be used to assess patterns operating in your life right now—or patterns that may influence you six months or fifty years from now. Transits, daily motions of the planets, have the most immediate and obvious effect, particularly when the slow-moving planets Pluto, Neptune, and Uranus are involved. The longer a planet remains in a particular sign, the greater its impact on us as individuals, a society, a country, a world.

"In Jungian terms, the astrological evidence suggests that the collective unconscious is ultimately embedded in the macrocosm itself, with the planetary motions a synchronistic reflection of the unfolding archetypal dynamics of the human experience," wrote Richard Tarnas in *Cosmos and Psyche: Intimations of a New World View*. Tarnas, like Grasse, considers these planetary archetypes to be intimately connected with myth.

Take Mars. In mythology, Mars was the Roman god of war. In astrology, he symbolizes physical and sexual energy, forward thrust, aggression, anger, and conflict. He represents our capacity to pursue what we desire, to conquer and defend. When Mars hits one of the planets or sensitive points in your birth chart, stuff happens. The nature of what happens depends on where or what Mars hits and the angle it makes to that planet or house.

Let's say Mars is moving through the sky (transiting) and comes to the same spot in the zodiac where the sun was positioned at the moment of your birth. The sun is the archetype of the self and symbolizes the totality of who you are. During the five or six weeks that Mars sits on top of your sun, your life becomes a study in chaos, speed, and action. Everything your solar archetype exemplifies becomes more pronounced, obvious, pressing. You may even feel more combative.

The zodiac consists of twelve signs, and each sign contains thirty degrees. The degree the sun occupied when you were born probably corresponds to a year in your life when some sort of transformative experience occurred—the birth of a sibling, a move, a parental divorce or remarriage, an accident, illness, or some other defining event. The timing isn't always exact—give it a leeway of about six months on either side. Trish, whose sun is at 16 degrees 12 minutes of Gemini, experienced a defining event five months after her sixteenth birthday. Her parents moved from Venezuela, where she had been born and raised, to the United States. That year she also discovered astrology, which helped to illuminate the ramifications of the move.

If your sun is positioned at, say, 25 degrees of your sign, you might meet your spouse at age twenty-five or your first child may be born. A sun at 8 degrees could mean your parents divorced when you were eight years old, or you were admitted to a gifted program in third grade that influenced the rest of your education.

In Reya's birth chart, the sun is at 24 degrees and 58 minutes of Aquarius (two minutes short of 25 degrees). When Trish first looked at her chart, she asked Reya what life-sculpting event happened to her between the ages of twenty-five and twenty-six. Just twelve days before her twenty-sixth birthday, Reya "was hit by a train and was unconscious for four days. That event took me out of a very destructive lifestyle into my first foray with alternative medicine," she wrote. "Could that be it?" You bet.

If you don't know the degree of your natal sun, go to *www.astro.com* for a free copy of your natal chart. Locate the sun—its symbol looks like a circle with a dot in the center. Next to it you will find numbers that indicate the degree of the sign in which your natal sun is placed. If you were born on October 14, 1950, for example, your sun would be in 20 degrees of Libra. This means there may have been a defining moment in your life when you were around twenty years old. Give it six months or so on either side. If you're not yet at the age that corresponds with the degree of your natal sun, keep in mind that some defining event may happen when you reach that age.

In *Cosmos and Psyche*, Richard Tarnas noted that transits of Uranus—the planet of innovation, genius, and sudden events—seem to coincide with periods of great discovery and creativity. For both Freud and Jung, their periods of greatest breakthrough and creativity took place when Uranus was opposed to the positions it occupied at their births. During such periods we become aware of our mortality and the years we have left on the planet. We seek freedom. Galileo, Descartes, and Newton also experienced monumental breakthroughs during Uranus oppositions. These men, says Tarnas, "all completed their revolutionary works when the transit was at its mathematical peak, within one or two degrees of exact alignment, something that with this transit occurs altogether for approximately twelve months in the course of a lifetime."

Ever wondered why your high school senior or college student is so rebellious? Blame Uranus. That's about the age when transiting Uranus forms a challenging angle with its natal position. When Maria (whom you met in Secret 5) was arrested for a DUI, Uranus was influencing her in a way that can signal disruptive, chaotic events that seem to come out of the blue.

If astrology as a divination technique interests you, you'll find plenty of websites that provide free natal charts, list daily transits, and explain what it all means. If you're looking for quick answers astrology can be daunting. However, its language, like that of the *I Ching*, can yield a surprising amount of information if you're willing to pursue it.

Tarot

Whereas the *I Ching* is chatty and astrology is a symbolic language, the tarot is hauntingly visual. The seventy-eight cards of the tarot are divided into two sections known as the major arcana and the minor arcana. The major arcana's twenty-two cards represent archetypes, specifically those of an evolution in consciousness. The Fool, the first card in the major arcana, symbolizes a peak moment, an intense euphoria that rises from the knowledge that we're all connected to something larger than we had imagined. The Fool is Pocahontas when she sings about the color of the wind, and represents the beginning of the magnificent journey ahead of us. The last card, The World, ends the Fool's journey and suggests the goal has been reached. You're now the sage, the master. The other fifty-six cards, the minor arcana, represent the synchronistic details of our lives and the steps along the path from The Fool to The World.

Robert Hopcke relates a humorous story about one of his clients who received a deck of tarot cards for her birthday. She initially used the deck with a "give-me-an-answer" attitude. One day she received an answer she disliked and drew the cards again, but all of the cards were reversed, "that is, facing away from her, as if they didn't want to talk to her. In synchronistic events like this one," Hopcke writes, "it almost seems that the cards had a will of their own."

Shortly after 9/11, Trish's coauthor for *Power Tarot*, Phyllis Vega, remarked that nearly every client she'd read for lately seemed to be drawing The Tower. This card usually depicts a tower being struck by lightning. Flames shoot from its windows, people are falling or leaping to their deaths, everything is dark, ugly, terrifying. If there's any card that depicts the scenario of 9/11, this is it. In the months following the disaster, the archetypes of destruction, chaos, and death became embedded in our collective psyche as a nation. The Tower card reflected it.

Whenever you draw The Tower in a personal reading, the archetype generally points to chaos—not destruction and death in the physical sense. Often the chaos catches you by surprise. Let's say you pull The Tower card several times in the days just before you're leaving for vacation— and it comes up when you ask questions that have nothing to do with your vacation. It may be indicating problems with your trip, so it would be wise to recheck your itinerary and ticket, leave for the airport earlier than usual, and be sure you've packed everything you need. If you have a lengthy drive to the airport, be sure your car is in shape—oil changed, gas tank full, engine humming.

The tarot, like astrology and the *I Ching*, probably isn't the simplest divination system. If you want to engage synchronicity quickly, try stichomancy.

YOU AND THE TAROT

To familiarize yourself with the tarot, draw a card each morning to get a sense of your day. Start off using just the major arcana cards. Allow the image to speak to the deeper part of you, then check your impressions with the meanings in a tarot book. As you learn the meanings of the cards, use the entire deck.

Let's say your card for the day is The Chariot. This would indicate that you may be on the road more that day—perhaps running errands, commuting to work. It could also mean that an issue or situation comes to a head and you triumph.

You can also "open" a card by drawing a second one to glean more information. If you drew the three of cups with The Chariot, for instance, then your day would be filled with celebration.

Be sure to have a tarot book that provides meanings for the cards that are easy to understand.

Stichomancy

This system is quick and easy—and amazingly accurate. Think of a question or issue that concerns you. Hold it in your mind, open any book at random, and point to a place on the page. See if the word or phrase your finger touches illuminates your question or concern.

Just about any book will do: a dictionary, the Bible or other religious text, *Grimms' Fairy Tales*, your favorite novel or nonfiction book, even a magazine will do. The larger the book, the more possible answers you'll have. The symbology of the source you use should also resonate for you. In other words, if you're not familiar with the Bible, that probably wouldn't be the ideal book to use. You can also try this online, by navigating to any of the many sites that provide stichomancy readings.

Let's say you're a fairy tale buff and are conversant in the symbology of these stories. Think of your question, open the Brothers Grimm at random, and then with your eyes closed, point at any spot on the page. The word, phrase, or sentence your finger touches should address your question. For additional insight, take note of the particular fairy tale.

Maybe you asked where a romantic relationship is going and pointed at the word "think" in the story about the big bad wolf. This could be an indication that you should rethink the relationship because something about your partner may be deceptive. The person's values may be skewed in some way.

Suppose you asked if you're going to get the promotion you want and pointed at a blank space in *Snow White*. This could suggest the answer is unknown right now or that your promotion will come through in the winter. If you get an ambiguous answer, try again and phrase your question differently. Or, when you point at a word, read the entire sentence or paragraph. If you landed on a sentence where Snow White pricks her finger with a needle and three drops of blood fall upon the snow, this could mean you'll hear about the promotion in three minutes, days, or weeks—or during the winter months.

A dictionary is probably the fastest way to peek at the enfolded order in your life. For example, Rob posed the question: What are the benefits of divination? He opened the dictionary and dropped his finger at a page. The words he pointed to were: *To wish longingly, or intently.* A reasonable response. When looking for a peek at the future, we're often wishing for a particular outcome. That response could even reveal a bit of humor or irony, as if the universe was saying that divination was wishful thinking. But then, where did *that* answer come from?

If you're sitting in a doctor or dentist's office and have a question that needs an immediate answer, choose the thickest magazine you can find. Open it and point. If your finger lands on an advertisement, see if there's anything about it or the product or the other images that resonate with you. If not, try again and rephrase your question so it's more specific.

Your Inner Oracle

The beauty of divination systems is that there are so many. They all work on similar principles and can bring you to the same place—that point of connection between the inner and external worlds, the space between.

If you're oriented toward color, consider creating your own oracle with colored squares made of cardboard or heavy paper. Colors, like the images in the tarot, reflect archetypal meanings. Yet, there is a subtle difference. Color is immediate, familiar, and everywhere. It constantly affects us and therefore makes an ideal oracle.

Make sure the squares are exactly the same size and that the colors are visible on only one side. That way you can shuffle and select squares without knowing which colors you're choosing. Assign meanings to the different colors. Start with the three primary colors red, blue, yellow, then black and white. Add more colors—purple or violet, gold, orange, and green. Assign meanings to these, too. Come up with twelve to fifteen colors and give all of them meanings.

If you're not sure what colors mean, look on the Internet for suggestions. Colors have psychological, cultural, and personal associations. Pick the ones that feel right for you. Here are some possible interpretations from *The Rainbow Oracle:*

The Book of Color Divination that Rob coauthored with Tony Grosso.

- Red: Passion, intensity, ardent enthusiasm, heightened physical and emotional energy
- Orange: Harmony, balance between the mind and emotions
- Yellow: Learning, intellect, logic, legal documents, order
- Green: Change, growth, healing, renewal, money, birth, new ideas
- Blue: Serenity, tranquility, sensitivity, devotion, introversion, privacy
- Purple: Rules and regulations, tradition, the past, the romantic
- Violet: Higher awareness, spirituality, wisdom, love of humanity, idealism
- Pink: Tenderness, gentle love, maintaining health, sensitivity, vitality
- Brown: Solid foundations, fertility, security, stability
- Peach: Balance, mellowness, happiness
- Gold: Success, creative thought, attainment of goals, positive thinking
- Silver: Versatility, flexibility, intuition, psychic awareness
- Gray: Confusion and misunderstanding, despondency, fear
- White: Insightful awareness, realization, protection, understanding achieved through clear and positive thinking
- Black: Something not presently understood or revealed, hidden thoughts, feelings, or actions

Personalize the meanings of the colors. Maybe instead of high energy, red to you means stop, danger. Once you have determined your color meanings, create a couple of "spreads," perhaps using common tarot spreads as models. Some of the best spreads are the simplest. First, pose your question, select the appropriate spread, then shuffle the colored cards, and lay them out according to the spread.

Here are some examples:

PAST, PRESENT, FUTURE SPREAD

1	2	3
Past	Present	Future

WHAT MAY BE BLOCKING YOU SPREAD

1	2	3	4
The issue	Hidden potential	Challenge/obstacle	Resolution

OVERVIEW SPREAD (YOU DETERMINE THE TIME FRAME)

1	2	3	4	5	6	7
Main issue	Finances	Home	Life	Love/ romance	Career	Your course of action

If you have at least twelve to fifteen cards to work with, you can design longer spreads that use more cards. The following spread is based on astrology and provides a lot of information. Set a time frame for your question or concern—a week, two months, six months.

ASTROLOGY SPREAD

1	2	3	4	5	6
Self	Finances	Communication	Home	Creativity	Work / health

ASTROLOGY SPREAD

7	8	9	10	11	12	13
Partnerships	Shared resources	Travel	Career	Friends	What's hidden; overview of question	The overview

Divination systems trigger synchronicity, and sometimes the results are so direct they take your breath away. Whatever divination system you work with, even if you merely open a dictionary and point, you're embarking on a journey into the oneness of the universe. As Robert Hopcke wrote, "Divinatory methods allow us to use the very same capacity as we use to create art, write fiction or imagine anything significant into being."

QUICK AND EASY DIVINATION

Granted, not everyone who is interested in synchronicities will rush out to buy a deck of tarot cards, study the *I Ching*, or have her astrological chart cast. However, simple divination tools are at your disposal 24/7.

Pose your question, then instead of consulting a book simply tell yourself that the next thing you hear, see, or read will provide an answer. Maybe your answer comes through a song on the radio or the first words your partner speaks to you in the morning. Maybe the answer lies in the headline of the morning paper, or something said on television. Play with the information. Roll it around in your mind. How does it fit your question? If you can't find any connection, drop it and look for the next possibility. If that doesn't work, it could indicate you're not meant to receive an answer now. It also could suggest you don't want to accept the answer that was presented to you.

Wait an hour or a day, then try again. One way or another, you *will* get your answer.

ANIMAL ORACLES

"Everyone has been touched by animals in some way, either in life or in dreams, and always the difficulty is determining what it means."

—TED ANDREWS, *ANIMAL-WISE*

In late December of 2004, an undersea earthquake erupted in the Indian Ocean. The violent upheaval of the tectonic plates displaced an enormous amount of water and within a few hours, waves as high as a hundred feet radiated outward from the epicenter. A tsunami crashed into the coastline of eleven Indian Ocean countries, killing more than 250,000 people.

Because the wave that spread out across the Bay of Bengal was visible from space, scientists could precisely measure the size of the quake and the resulting tsunami. However, they were unable to predict it. What became apparent from the earliest reports—and in information gathered during the years since—is that animals were aware of the eruption hours, even days, in advance.

On January 11, 2005, an online article in *National Geographic* featured numerous stories about animals that had survived the tsunami. Giant waves washed floodwaters up to two miles inland at Yala National Park in Sri Lanka's biggest wildlife reserve, home to hundreds of elephants, buffalo, leopards, deer, jackals, and monkeys. Yet, the deputy director of the National Wildlife Department, R. D. Ratnayake, said there were no reports of dead animals. "The elephants, wild boar, deer, monkeys, and others moved inland to avoid the killer waves."

Survivors described how monkeys, who always accept bananas, rejected them on the morning of the tsunami; how elephants screamed and fled to higher ground; how dogs refused to go on their usual morning walks. Even a pair of tethered elephants pulled free of their chains and ran to higher ground for safety before the tsunami crashed against the shore. Flamingos that breed at that time of year at the Point Calimere wildlife sanctuary in India flew to higher ground beforehand and abandoned their breeding grounds.

Ravi Corea, president of the Sri Lanka Wildlife Conservation Society, based in Nutley, New Jersey, was in Sri Lanka when the massive waves struck. Afterward, he traveled to the Patanangala beach inside Yala National Park, where sixty visitors were washed away. The beach was one of the worst-hit areas of the 500-square-mile wildlife reserve, which is home to a variety of animals, including elephants, leopards, and 130 species of birds. Other than two water buffalo that died, Corea didn't see any animal carcasses, nor did the park personnel know of any.

Along India's Cuddalore coast, where thousands of people perished, the Indo-Asian News Service reported that buffaloes, goats, and dogs were found unharmed. Another survivor recalled bats frantically flying away just before the tsunami struck. In Thailand, a dolphin and her calf reportedly got caught in a lagoon after the tsunami, but many other dolphins fled.

The anecdotes are numerous and involve a variety of species. They clearly show that animals sensed the tsunami's approach and vacated the area.

"Imagine what could happen . . . if, instead of ignoring the warnings given by animals, people took them seriously," wrote British biologist Rupert Sheldrake in *Dogs That Know When Their Owners Are Coming Home.*

On May 12, 2008, China experienced its worst earthquake in three decades, a 7.9 in the Sichuan Province. Three weeks before the quake, in a province 350 miles from the quake's epicenter, the water level in a pond suddenly plunged. Three days before the quake, thousands of toads appeared in the streets of Mianzhu. Residents feared the toads were a sign of an approaching natural disaster. But according to an AP story, an official with the local forestry bureau quashed this theory by saying the toad behavior was normal.

On the day of the quake, zebras at a zoo in Wuhan, more than 600 miles from the quake's epicenter, banged their heads against doors. Elephants trunks swung wildly and lions and tigers paced restlessly. Five minutes before the quake hit, peacocks started screeching.

Sheldrake noted that before an earthquake on September 26, 1997 that obliterated the Basilica of St. Francis in Assisi, Italy, there were numerous reports of animals acting strangely. Dogs barked more than usual, cats seemed "disturbed," pigeons "flew strangely," and pheasants "screamed in an unusual way." At least a week before the earthquake, people in Foligno, twelve miles from Assisi, reported rats invading the town.

In some instances, authorities have successfully forecast major earthquakes based in part on their observation of the strange antics of animals. *National Geographic* reported that in 1975, Chinese officials ordered the evacuation of Haicheng, a city with one million people, just days before a 7.3-magnitude quake. Only a small portion of the population was hurt or killed. If the city officials had ignored the odd animal behavior, it's estimated that the number of fatalities and injuries could have exceeded 150,000.

According to the U.S. Geological Survey, accounts of animals acting strangely before earthquakes date back to Greece in 373 B.C., when rats, weasels, snakes, and centipedes supposedly left their homes and headed for safety several days before a destructive earthquake. Pliny the Elder, who lived between A.D. 23 and 79, wrote that one of the signs of an impending quake "is the excitation and terror of animals with no apparent reason."

Sheldrake put forth four theories about how animals know, and refuted the first three: They are able to detect what we cannot—subtle sounds, vibrations, movements of the earth; they sense gases released by the earth prior to earthquakes; they respond to electrical changes that precede an earthquake. His fourth theory states "animals may sense what is about to happen in a way that lies beyond our current scientific under-standing. In other words, they may be presentient, having a feeling that something is about to happen, or precognitive, knowing in advance what is going to happen."

There is plenty of evidence of animals predicting earth-quakes. Can they also act as early warning systems for other natural disasters? And if so, how can this knowledge benefit us?

During 2004, Florida was hit by three hurricanes: Frances, Charlie, and Jeanne. Birds apparently delayed their migration while the storms churned through Florida. When Hurricane Jeanne was still several hours away from Gainesville, Univer-sity of Florida biologist Thomas Emmel noticed the butterflies in the university's enclosed rainforest took shelter among the rocks and trees. When Hurricane Charlie was within twelve hours of southwest Florida, scientists at the Mote Marine Laboratory near Sarasota, Florida, noticed the odd behavior among ten tiger sharks they had tagged. Eight of them fled the estuary for the safety of the open ocean. In 1992, Hurricane Andrew slammed into Homestead, Florida, and wiped it off the map. In its path was the habitat of crocodiles that live in the cooling canals of the Turkey Point nuclear power plant. Apparently the crocodiles sensed the approach of the storm; once it had moved on, not a single dead crocodile was found. It's speculated that they fled into open water or to the bottom of the twenty-foot canals.

"It doesn't make any difference if it's a hurricane, a fire, or an earthquake," said Frank Mazzotti, a wildlife biologist at the University of Florida. "They apparently sense these things before humans can do that. Not a lot of work has been done to learn the sensory mechanisms. It's likely a combination of smell, vibrations, and pressure. They start moving away from danger before humans pick it up."

Animals as Symbols

Animals are among the most accessible synchronistic symbols and you don't have to live in a rural area to experience animals as messengers or guides. Joseph Campbell, after all, lived on the fourteenth floor of a Manhattan building when he experienced his praying mantis synchronicity (discussed in Secret 1).

Ray Grasse, author of *The Waking Dream*, recalled how the erratic flight of a bird provided a clue to understanding a question on his mind. The author was involved in a lengthy discussion with a native healer in Arizona, when the man suggested they take a walk along the edge of the village where they could look out over the desert. The medicine man asked Grasse about his life and Grasse mentioned a project he would start soon. He noted that the effort seemed to be taking a direction he hadn't intended. At that moment, a bird darted in front of them, let out a cry, and turned sharply. "See!" said the medicine man. "There you are! Like you thought, things are going to turn out quite differently than you originally planned." The healer explained that messages are presented to us all the time, but most people have forgotten how to read them.

Grasse's story illustrates how clear an animal's message can be once you understand which animals speak to you and what they're conveying. Any creature may be a messenger, a vehicle for synchronicity. Whether you call these animals oracles or totems, their presence in your life links you to ancient shamanic traditions, to a world more natural than the one in which most of us now live.

When an animal appears to you—especially one you wouldn't normally see in the course of your ordinary day, or that shows up under unusual circumstances—consider what you were thinking about or doing at the time. The sighting could be a verification that you're making the right decision, as in Grasse's case. The animal's appearance or its actions could warn you that you're about to make a bad decision.

If you're paying attention, you'll notice that different animals may appear synchronistically at different times, for specific reasons. The reason may not always be apparent to you at the time, but you'll intuitively feel the connection. You could call that creature your power animal, spirit animal, or totem, and draw on the energy it offers.

FINDING YOUR POWER ANIMAL

This meditation helps you find your power or spirit animal. Sit in a comfortable chair in a quiet setting. Keep your back straight and take several deep breaths to gradually still your mind, then soften your breathing so it feels natural. Let your thoughts drift for a few moments, until your daily concerns no longer seem pressing.

Know that you are protected as you sink deeper into a relaxed state. Imagine a beautiful place in nature—a trail in a majestic forest with sunshine beaming through the canopy, or a spot by a stream or waterfall with mountains in the distance. Put yourself in this place. Sense your surroundings, the sounds and smells of nature.

Call to your animal guardian, even if you don't know what it is yet. Sense the animal approaching, coming toward you. You feel safe and secure as it moves closer. Now you can see the animal clearly. Is it furry, feathery, small, large? Look into its eyes and feel a connection with the animal.

The creature has a message for you. You may hear the message as a voice in your head, or the animal's actions may communicate the message symbolically. After a few moments, thank the creature for its guidance. Know that you can go back again to visit your power animal whenever you choose.

If you already know your power animal, you can call on it for help or healing or anything else you may need. Jane Clifford of Wales considers the swan her power animal. She called on it one morning when she woke feeling blue and out of sorts—the words "the Lord is my Shepherd" kept running through her head. "I felt so low that for the first time, I called on swan to help out. I opened my eyes and to my absolute astonishment, two swans flew past." Although she'd lived in a riverside house for two years, this was the first time she'd seen swans in flight. For a moment, she doubted the experience, wondering if she'd imagined it. "In answer, they flew past again the opposite way."

Consider a question or matter that concerns you, then during the day watch for the appearance of an animal. If you have pets, exclude them for this divinatory exercise, because they are a constant in your life.

We've provided a short list of animals and their possible synchronistic meanings. Many excellent books exist on this subject, and numerous online sites offer more informa-tion. When you experience an animal synchronicity—either in real life or in a dream—trust your own impressions and interpretations. What does the animal mean to you? How is it significant in your life?

Research the animal for possible clues to its message. What do its habitat, physical characteristics, behavior, and habits tell you? Is it a mammal, bird, reptile, fish, or insect? What are its most recognized qualities? Where does it live?

How long is the female pregnant? Does it give live birth or lay eggs? Does it mate for life? Is it nomadic? Predator or prey? Endangered? All of this information provides you with vital clues about what your animal synchronicity might mean.

Birds as Messengers and Oracles

In a broad sense, all birds are messengers. So many species of birds exist, they could comprise their own book of oracles. We've listed some of the more common birds. Use these meanings only as guidelines to come up with your own interpretations.

Blackbird (red-winged, grackle, meadowlark)

Time to socialize. You may have to dig around for the information you need, and the first place to start is with other people. Someone in your circle of acquaintances may have expertise or skills that can help you.

Buzzard

Known as a scavenger bird, buzzards or vultures serve to rid the environment of decaying remains of animals. What do you need to clean up in your life? Which loose ends are waiting to be tied up?

Canary

Miners took canaries down into the shafts to provide early warnings of dangerous gases in the air. The appearance of a canary might signify a warning. Note the details surrounding your sighting or dream of this bird. Don't judge people by the way they look.

Condor

Seeing this endangered bird indicates you need to see the bigger picture. But don't place yourself in jeopardy to get that broader perspective.

Crow

Like his brother the raven, the crow is often believed to convey messages between the dead and the living and is linked with birth and rebirth. He's associated with shamanic magic, too. When you have a synchronistic encounter with a crow, the message might be that you should work more diligently at manifesting your desires. Also, try to be more open to the concept of reincarnation.

Dove

You're not just looking for a committed relationship, you're searching for your soul mate. We associate doves with peace. Therefore, if you see a dove and you're concerned about a relationship issue, the bird's appearance could indicate that a relationship issue will be resolved, peacefully.

Eagle

Seeing an eagle encourages you to use your intuition. Like the eagle, there's something regal about you and the way you do things. You enjoy the company of others; however, someone with whom you're involved may have a better reputation than he or she deserves. You're able to see the bigger picture—the bird's-eye view.

Hawk

Grace and agility are your strengths. You're looking for the broader perspective. Get out and socialize; don't be such a loner. Be vigilant for predatory practices.

Hummingbird

Long-distance travel is in your future. So are joy, celebration, and love. This animal synchronicity usually points to something positive.

Owl

Across time, borders, and cultures, the mythology and folklore about owls involves extremes. They've been tagged as harbingers of death and of healing, of unspeakable evil and of great wisdom. In Celtic tradition, owls symbolize the underworld. Zulus consider the owl to be the sorcerer's bird. In Peru, owls are thought to be strong shamanic medicine. Among Australian Aborigines, they're believed to be the souls of women. In Siberia, the owl is considered a helpful spirit.

The long tradition of owls as messengers is beautifully illustrated in the Harry Potter books and movies. Remember the opening scenes in the first movie? Owls sweep into the main hall and drop letters down over the students. They are literally mail carriers who freely traverse the boundary between the mundane world and the magical world of Hogwarts. In many shamanic traditions, owls are believed to move between the worlds of the living and the dead with ease, equally at home in both realms.

Sometimes owls are viewed as harbingers of death. One afternoon Trish saw an owl perched on the fence outside her dad's window. In his mid-nineties at the time, her father had Parkinson's and was struggling to adjust to the fact that his wife of fifty years was in an Alzheimer's facility.

She went outside for a closer look at the bird. It was a burrowing owl, an endangered species with ground nests. It didn't fly away as she approached and she saw that it was missing part of its left leg. That puzzled her. Her dad had both his legs and used a cane to get around. If the owl was a symbol of his imminent death, what was the owl's missing leg about?

The next morning, she received a call from the Alzheimer's facility where her mother resided and was told her mother had broken her left hip. The owl was missing part of its left leg. Due to the Alzheimer's, Trish's mom wasn't eligible for hip replacement surgery. The alternative was morphine and a nursing home. Three weeks later, her mother died.

Swan

Swans mate for life. Seeing this bird suggests that you should trust the process. A romance may quickly turn into a lifelong committed relationship.

Invertebrates as Messengers and Oracles

Invertebrates are so common that you could drive yourself nuts trying to figure out the message every time you see one. But if you're stung, or your house suddenly fills with these critters, you should pay attention.

Ant

You're feeling restless, antsy. Your schedule is jammed and you could be in danger of becoming a workaholic. If you love what you do, that's fine. You may feel you're working for the greater good. Otherwise, the ant's message may be to assess your work situation.

Bee
The specific message depends on the type of bee. The honeybee symbolizes generosity, teamwork, and a sweetness of spirit. The bumblebee represents communication and healing.

Butterfly
Seeing a butterfly may herald a transformation, resurrection, or rebirth of some kind. Expect profound changes in your life, in your relationships, career, family, or another area.

Caterpillar
Like the butterfly, caterpillars are linked with transformation. Your life is about to undergo a transformation that will enable you to break out and show who you really are.

Dragonfly
Good news is on the way. These beautiful creatures often symbolize good luck.

Firefly
You're in search of the truth. Your inner radiance lights up the darkness and garners you attention   your brilliance might even attract the ideal partner.

Ladybug
Seeing a ladybug suggests good luck, transformation, and joy. It urges you to pay attention to family life and spiritual considerations.

Spider
Look forward to a powerful creative period. Camouflage and patience can serve you well.

Wasp
This insect represents independence and self-sufficiency. If a wasp stings you, it may be time to determine where and how you feel injured in your life. Heal the wound through forgiveness.

Amphibians and Reptiles as Messengers and Oracles

While it is hard to accurately summarize this category of creatures, as they mean very different things, it's still worthwhile to pay attention to their presence in your life to become attuned to how it may apply.

Frog
In myth, folklore, and fairy tales, the frog is a symbol of transformation, healing, fertility, and renewal. It represents the trickster and magician archetypes, the cycle of death and rebirth. In the fairy tale *The Frog Prince* by the Brothers Grimm a princess is wooed by a frog who asks for a kiss. Initially horrified by the request, the princess gradually consents out of pity. The moment she kisses the ugly frog, he's transformed into a prince. The two are married, of course, and the moral of the tale is that beauty is only skin deep.

The frog's rich shamanic history draws upon its alchemical qualities. Frogs and toads are purveyors of poison and powerful drugs, which can heal or induce hallucinations. Some South American tribes use toad and frog poisons in their spiritual rituals as part of vision quests. The chemical secreted by the poison dart frog can be useful as a cardiac stimulant for heart attack patients, but also produces a painkiller that may someday replace morphine. Thus, symbolism involving a frog usually contains at least two facets.

Frogs are an "indicator species," meaning they are among the first to be affected by changes in the environment. So when frogs appear to us as symbols, it might mean our personal environments are about to undergo major changes.

In *The Dreaming Universe*, physicist Fred Alan Wolf related a story of a therapist whose patient, a young girl, was so ill her doctors didn't think she would live through the night. The therapist, Catherine, visited the comatose girl at the hospital and started talking to her, telling her she could "go into a vast open space and that the space would be enough to keep the girl comfortable. Catherine did not tell her what the space would be like or what she would see in the space. Catherine was leaving it open so that something could happen purely initiated by the girl herself."

Within a short period of time, the girl came out of her coma, sat up, and said, "The frog jumps." Then she dropped back on the bed and went to sleep. By the next morning, she was on the road to recovery.

When Catherine went to the hospital the next day, she stopped in the gift shop and bought a toy frog for the girl. "I gave it to her because she needed something very concrete to recognize that her image had brought her back to life."

Only later did Catherine discover that the frog, as a symbol, had an illustrious history "involving sick children and was given to children who needed to believe in life."

If frogs are one of your totems, the synchronistic appearance of a frog alerts you that something significant is headed your way. Whether it's good luck or bad depends on the condition of the frog. If the frog is injured or dead, the news or event may not be positive. A lively leaping frog could indicate good news bounding your way, a fresh start, even a transformation.

Lizard

This animal reminds you to set your own pace, be observant, and camouflage yourself. Let people come to you.

Snake

Your sexuality is heightened. And, perhaps paradoxically, so is your spirituality. By shedding relationships, beliefs, and situations that are no longer in your best interest, your personal power increases.

Turtle

Numerous opportunities are headed your way. Take your time sifting through them. Follow your instincts about choosing the opportunity that is right for you.

Mammals as Messengers and Oracles

Mammals are all around you, so becoming alert to their special significance in your life can open a window onto even greater synchronicities all around you.

Cat

A cat brings a message that your sleeping habits are about to change. Maybe you'll sleep more during the day, leaving the night open for creative work and exploration. Or perhaps you're going to start working the night shift. More independence and solitude are beneficial now. Don't worry about what other people think.

Deer

Deer have long been associated with grace and camouflage. When one synchronistically appears in your life, it may indicate you'll be required to adapt to a situation or within a relationship. For Jenean Gilstrap, a synchronicity involving a deer brought home the need to end a relationship.

"A few years ago, in the midst of a fantastic, cosmic personal relationship, I was questioning the logic/validity of my continuing this relationship regardless of how much I wanted to stay."

At some level, Jenean had always known the time would come when she would have to decide whether to stay or leave. She struggled daily with the issue. "Driving the long highway to work one cold morning, I began another mental dialogue— stay or go, go or stay—and mentally phrased a request for a sign of what I must do—just something, anything, to help me see my way more clearly."

With that thought, while driving in the left lane of a four-lane highway in a commercially developed area, she glanced down briefly. Then she looked up again. "There, directly in front of me, was the face of a deer, looking me straight in the eye. Her head was even with mine and her eyes turned directly to me as she bounded across my path and onto the median of grass."

It seemed so surreal Jenean was certain she'd imagined it. Logistically, it wasn't possible for the deer to be in midair in front of her as she traveled in the left lane with another car parallel to her in the right lane. But she glanced in her side mirror and saw the deer bounding down the median.

The same conversation ran through Jenean's mind as she drove to work a few days later. The night before she'd had a dream in which her lover had died and she'd seen him in his casket. "So as I'm driving with the mental image of his casket in my mind, still questioning, asking for a sign, for assurance, I approached the same place on the road where the earlier deer had jumped in front of my car. There, on the side of the road, was a dead deer. A doe."

Could the message be any clearer? She ended the relationship shortly afterward.

Dog

The tail wagging, the slobbering kisses when you walk in your front door: dogs symbolize unconditional love and acceptance. No wonder so many of us believe our dogs understand us better than our human partners. Like other animals, they can also serve as oracles, as vehicles for synchronicities and transformations.

On her way to work one day, Vivian Ortiz, a psychiatric ER nurse in Savannah, saw a dog wandering through traffic. Thin, confused, it was ripe for extinction among the speeding cars. She stopped and coaxed the dog, a beagle mix, into her car, then took it to her vet. Vivian subsequently adopted the dog, which she named Sister, and was delighted that the stray got along well with her cats.

A year later, Vivian, who lives alone, was on her way to work and saw another dog in the same predicament, on the same road; again, she stopped and coaxed it into her car. A homeless man nearby called out his thanks to her for doing the right thing. The dog was a beagle mix, a male. Now Sister and Brother are the best of friends, keeping each other company while Vivian is at work. From the point of view of those two dogs, Vivian served as an oracle, a symbol of transformation for their lives. In return, their unconditional love for Vivan has enriched her life.

Dolphin

Dolphins call you to pay attention to your dream life and spirituality. At this time you'll achieve the most within a group or working with a team of like-minded individuals. In some way, you're protected. For now, sex is just for fun.

Mouse

The devil is in the details, as the saying goes. Seeing a mouse reminds you to connect the dots, save something for the future, but don't accumulate so much stuff that you're bogged down.

Squirrel

Squirrels represent communication. They also can advise resourcefulness, storing, and planning for the future.

YOUR ANIMAL GLOSSARY

Some of these meanings may fit your experiences. It's likely you'll discover that many of your own animal experiences mean something different. If you're terrified of dogs, for example, you probably won't associate them with unconditional love and acceptance. For you, it may be an omen that something frightening is coming into your life. Keep track of your animal experiences and the synchronicities that unfold. Use your insights to create your own glossary.

JOURNEYS

"Beyond the obvious increased opportunities it provides for encountering meaningful coincidences, travel is itself a transformational experience."

—FRANK JOSEPH, *SYNCHRONICITY & YOU*

Whether you're headed across town or across the world, travel removes you from normal routines and habitual thinking. You're open to new experiences, uncanny encounters, and all the high strangeness the universe can muster.

Most of us set out with a checklist for routine trips across town and plan an itinerary for longer journeys. But along the way, stuff happens. The car breaks down. The connecting flight is cancelled and you end up in Atlanta instead of Albuquerque. If you've left large chunks of your trip unstructured you have time for exploration. That's when it gets interesting, when you have a chance to engage synchronicity. Suddenly, running into the same people again and again isn't just an oddity; it's an opportunity to decipher and use the message. Why these people? Is your journey being hindered or facilitated?

Chance Encounters

An unlikely encounter helped author Richard Bach find a missing part for a rare airplane. As Bach related in *Nothing by Chance*, in 1966 he was barnstorming the Midwest in a rare biplane, a 1929 Detroit-Parks P-2A Speedster; only eight were ever built. In Palmyra, Wisconsin, Bach loaned the plane to a friend, who flipped it over upon landing. The damage was minor and the two men were able to fix everything except one strut. That repair looked hopeless because the part was custom-made.

Just then, the owner of the hangar approached them, asked if he could help, and offered to let them have any of the parts stored in his three hangars. When Bach described the rare part he needed, the man walked over to a nearby pile of junk and pointed to the exact part.

Bach concluded, "The odds against our breaking the biplane in a little town that happened to be home to a man with the forty-year-old part to repair it; the odds that he would be on the scene when the event happened; the odds that we'd push the plane right next to his hangar, within ten feet of the part we needed—the odds were so high that coincidence was a foolish answer."

This kind of experience is exactly what can happen when you remove yourself from your ordinary routines. Free of the need to keep a schedule, to put in eight hours a day at work, to cook, take out the garbage, drive the kids to and from school, you throw open your arms to embrace whatever comes your way. Suddenly the law of attraction works seamlessly.

TRAVEL TIPS

You can take certain steps before you leave home and during your trip to encourage synchronicity as you travel.

1. Be open and receptive to new experiences. Make sure your itinerary leaves room for side trips, detours, and surprises. If you're supposed to be in Athens on the fourth day of your trip through Greece, but hear of an intriguing opportunity to travel to Mykonos, make adjustments so you don't miss out on something amazing.
2. Cultivate an attitude of nonresistance. Instead of fuming about the slow security line at the airport, be observant. Notice the people around you and their mini-dramas. Read a book. Check your e-mail.
3. Go with the flow. If you're traveling with another person who really wants to see Stonehenge, but it doesn't

particularly interest you, go anyway. Synchronicity may be waiting for you there.

4. Intuition often speaks through impulses. If you have an impulse to stay a day longer at a destination, follow it. See where it leads.

5. Approach travel as an adventure. Seek new experiences. Don't hesitate to try new things.

When Jennifer Gerard lived in Japan, she was open to any and all new experiences. One day she went to a street psychic who read the bumps on her head, an event that probably changed the course of her life.

He told her Nepal would be a good country for her. She didn't know anything about Nepal, had no plans to travel there. But she wanted to go to China and take the Trans-Siberian Railway across Mongolia to Europe. A year later, she traveled to China with a friend. En route, they met a couple of guys. Without any planning, they ran into the same two young men in two other cities in China, an immense country with the largest population on the planet. "What were the chances that we would meet them three times, hundreds of miles apart?" she wondered.

They decided journeying together must be destined, so they traveled all over China with the young men. They planned to take the Trans-Siberian Railway together, but when they arrived in Beijing, they were told there had been some political trouble at the border. A trip to Europe via the railway wouldn't be possible for months. One of Jennifer's companions picked up a brochure about Nepal and read "kayaking" and "great food." They decided to go overland through China to Tibet and Nepal.

Jennifer describes the journey as difficult, but fantastic. In Nepal they parted amicably, for no particular reason. "It was as if these young men chaperoned me to the place where my new life began. Certainly, I would not have traveled as far as I did without one of the young men, a Scotsman fluent in Mandarin Chinese. On that trip, without any real planning, I started a business from Nepal and I have been going back regularly ever since." Jennifer now sells jewelry and other crafts made in Nepal, which she collects on her annual trips to that country.

During her first trip to Nepal, she found a Salagrama in a riverbed. This black rock, when split open, reveals a fossilized ammonite, a spiral with radiating lines, hiding inside. "In Nepal it is believed that when you find a Salagrama, it means that you are on your correct path in life." From the reading of the bumps on her head to the discovery of the Salagrama, the synchronicity had come full circle.

TRAVEL SYNCHRONICITY PRACTICE

Synchronicities are a great hook for recording your travel experiences. Start your day expecting synchronicity. After all, when you're on a journey, unexpected things happen.

Watch for chance encounters, but don't take chances you might regret. If you happen to engage in conversation with someone, pay attention to what the person says. A comment, phrase, even a single word could trigger an idea or a new option.

Unfortunately, difficulties and complications are often part of the typical travel scenario. Try to take advantage of the situation. Stay positive and see it as a new twist, another adventure. Frustration and tension can lead to new options and possibilities.

At the end of the day, jot down your thoughts about the day's events. Look for synchronicities and how unexpected incidents changed your path. Notice over time how one incident can build on another and another until your trip— and your life—have been altered in unexpected ways.

Some travel synchronicities are like mirrors, reflecting your immediate surroundings and circumstances in uncanny ways, but also with personal implications. In 1988, we were in Venezuela, where Trish was born and raised. On our way back from a visit to Angel Falls, we were in the Maiquetia airport that serves Caracas, standing in line to board our plane to the U.S. Guards armed with machine guns were everywhere. Colombian drug dealers had begun using Caracas to export cocaine and the government was cracking down.

The guards were particularly interested in the man in front of us, a tall, middle-aged Venezuelan in a three-piece suit, carrying a briefcase. They told him to open it. As the man slowly unlatched the briefcase, the guards leaned forward to see inside. The air crackled with tension.

We were standing right behind him and had a good view. Surprisingly, he carried only one item in the briefcase—a paperback copy of one of Trish's novels, *Fevered*. We were too stunned to let him in on the synchronicity. The odds that we would be standing behind this particular man, in the airport of the city where Trish had been born, and that his briefcase contained just one item—her book—are so outrageously high that even if we had let him in on the synchronicity, he probably wouldn't have believed it. And because the book was written under a pseudonym, Alison Drake, Trish wouldn't have been able to prove it anyway.

The book's title, *Fevered*, was a perfect reflection of the mood in the airport that day. The guards, the machine guns, the fear and suspicion. On a personal level, it was an affirmation for Trish that her books were reaching a larger audience.

Manifesting Travel Experiences

In 1996, Marcus Anthony, an Australian therapist-futurist and author, was visiting Coffs Harbour, a small Australian coastal town, when he followed intuitive nudges that led him into an astonishing experience that changed his life. Writing in *The Sage of Synchroncity*, Anthony described meeting a woman named Leslie who invited him to a meditation class in which she offered brief psychic reading for everyone. "She seemed to possess a type of mental ability that I had never encountered before . . . and I began to consider the possibility that human beings could 'see' beyond the five senses."

At the end of the session, Leslie said that she had dreamed about UFOs the previous night, and that if they went outside about two A.M., they might see something unusual. Even though he considered it highly unlikely that he would see a UFO, Anthony dragged himself out of bed at quarter to two. "My eyes almost popped out of my head when . . . five minutes later I saw a large ball of luminous white light . . . a few hundred meters in the air."

He watched it disappear over the neighboring house as it drifted toward the ocean. He ran down to the beach, and walked up and down the beach for an hour, but didn't see the object again. He returned to the house and took one more glance skyward. Directly above him were about twenty small red lights in a double V, one V inside the other. He watched in amazement for more than a minute as they moved silently by disappearing behind trees.

On his blog, Anthony wrote, "I have had quite a few interesting experiences since that day, but probably nothing quite so extraordinary as that night. Of all the things that set me on a path of questioning dominant knowledge structures of Western society . . . this experience was probably the most significant. What were those things I saw that night? How on earth did Leslie know that they were going to be there at that precise time, merely from a dream? Why are these kinds of phenomena still a taboo topic in modern science and academia? I'm still asking these questions today."

PRACTICE MANIFESTATION

Manifestation is one of the most challenging aspects of the law of attraction. The process has been laid out in numerous books, but the essence is simple: We get what we concentrate on. All too often, we focus on lack rather than on abundance. We look at the glass as half-empty.

When you travel, it's easier to manifest. Your needs are often immediate and pressing, and you're able to bypass your usual habitual thinking. Your desires soar away from you at such luminal speeds your psyche doesn't have a chance to throw up obstacles.

Here are some tips for honing your manifestation skills, on the road or at home:

1. State your desire aloud. Don't think too much about it, don't obsess about it. Just state it and release it, and remain open to your intuitive guidance.

2. Intuitive guidance comes in many shapes and sizes. An unknown person on the street may say exactly what you need to hear; a piece of paper that flutters at your feet might bring a message; words in a song that drifts through an open window could provide insight.

3. Believe your desire will manifest. Back your belief with powerful emotion. Act as if your desire has manifested already in your life. Feel the presence of that desire in your life. The stronger your emotion, the quicker the desire will manifest. This also works in reverse, of course. Negative emotion can attract negative synchronicities.

4. Once you've released your desire, get out of the way. Let the universe bring it to you. Don't keep checking your bank account, your relationship, your career for results. Let it be.

It's said that necessity is the mother of invention. When you're traveling, synchronicities are triggered by mundane needs, such as the location of a train station, shop, or restaurant. The desire to find what you need acts as a magnet for synchronicity.

During a business trip to Chicago, a synchronicity led Gabe Carlson exactly where he wanted to go. The owner of his company had recommended a restaurant called Tempo near his hotel. So Gabe and his coworkers, on their last morning in town, went looking for breakfast. But none of them could recall the name of the restaurant their boss had recommended. Gabe decided they should just walk "in a randomized direction," meaning a coworker who wasn't joining them would choose a direction and point. They walked off, Gabe said, bags in tow, "all smiles and openness to whatever goodness the universe and Chicago wanted to float our way."

After several blocks, it was obvious they weren't headed in the right direction. But they pressed on, hopeful. As they passed a McDonald's, a ragged homeless man approached Gabe and introduced himself as Andre. Gabe gave him some loose change, and the group continued on. A block later, they saw a deli. It didn't look promising, but they were hungry.

As they crossed the street, Andre loped after them, shouting that they shouldn't eat in the deli. "It's nasty," he said, claiming he knew of a better place. Several blocks later, Andre led them to Tempo, the café they had been seeking in the first place.

Some of us might have ignored the homeless man, but Gabe and his friends were open to whatever unfolded. They followed the cues and their search was rewarded.

As Jane Teresa Anderson noted in *The Shape of Things to Come*, "What comes up for us during our journey and challenges us to extend ourselves beyond our previous mental limitations meets us in the outer world through the mirror of synchronicity."

"Accidental" encounters with helpful people, such as the Chicago "bum" who led Gabe to the restaurant he sought, and the young man Jennifer Gerard met in China who spoke fluent Mandarin Chinese, are common during travel synchronicities. But other times, these encounters don't seem to have any rhyme or reason. That's how it was with a certain Australian Rob kept running into in Europe one summer.

The encounters began in Spain, where Rob and his traveling partner, Rabbit, continually bumped into an Aussie named Maurey. It seemed wherever they went, Maurey showed up. He wasn't particularly friendly and never seemed surprised to encounter them.

After three weeks in Spain, Rob and Rabbit headed for Morocco. They ferried to Ceuta and suddenly found themselves in a culture where they didn't speak the language and couldn't read the signs. They climbed into a hot, dusty bus with gaudy decor and claimed a couple of seats among the *jalaba*-clad Moroccans. Rob noticed two Western men three rows in front of them and elbowed Rabbit. "You aren't going to believe this," he said above the din of Arabic music and shouts of men arguing across the aisle. "There's Maurey."

They called out to him like he was a long-lost friend. Maurey and the guy next to him turned around. Rob and Rabbit were shocked to see that Maurey was sitting with Dave, a friend from Minneapolis, who was supposed to be traveling in Sweden, not Morocco. They had no idea that Dave planned to visit Morocco, yet here he was on their bus, sitting with Maurey.

What possible significance can this have? It wasn't as if Maurey proved helpful—he didn't speak the language and didn't have any more knowledge about the country than Rob or Rabbit. But if travel is a "journey toward growth," as authors Allan Combs and Mark Holland call it, perhaps these encounters with Maurey served to sharpen Rob's awareness of synchronicity. Maybe he was supposed to learn how to use such travel experiences as a compass.

Out-of-Body Journeys

And now for something completely different. An OBE, or out-of-body experience, is an exhilarating journey during which you leave your body behind. It can happen during an altered state of consciousness, while you're dreaming, meditating, or even under the influence of certain drugs. If you've ever suddenly jolted awake out of a seemingly real experience and were surprised to find yourself in bed, you could've been having an OBE. Exhilarating flying dreams, especially when you think you're awake, might also be OBEs. These experiences allow you to travel to distant places and later verify what you experienced.

In *Beyond the Quantum*, science writer Michael Talbot described an OBE from his teen years for which he was able to provide verifiable evidence. He first saw himself sleeping on his bed and everything looked normal. Then "I floated weightlessly out of my bedroom and into the living room, still marveling at the fact that all of the features of the house seemed identical to how I knew them in my waking state. . . . Suddenly, as I swam like some airborne fish through the rooms, I found myself heading on a collision course with a large picture window."

He didn't have time to panic—he drifted right through it. He floated outside, over the lawn and into another yard where he spotted a book in the grass. He moved closer and saw it was a collection of short stories by Guy de Maupassant. Although Michael had heard of the author, he didn't know the book or have any particular interest in it. After that, he lost his awareness and fell into a deep sleep.

The next morning on his way to school, a neighbor girl joined him and said she'd lost a library book—the very one he'd seen in his dream. Stunned, he related his experience and they strolled to the spot where he'd seen the book. "And there it was, nestled in the grass exactly as it had been when I had lazily floated over it."

Synchronicity? Yes. Clairvoyance or remote viewing? Yes. Proof of out-of-body travel? Maybe.

Robert Monroe, a Virginia businessman, recorded three decades of OBEs and wrote *Journeys Out of the Body*, the classic book on the subject. His experiences occurred spontaneously and he had no idea what was happening to him. He would lie down to go to sleep, and within minutes his body would shudder violently and he would feel as if he couldn't move. It took enormous willpower to force himself to wake up and break the grip of treacherous sleep. After several such experiences, he thought something was physically wrong with him, perhaps epilepsy or a brain tumor. However, his family doctor confirmed he was in perfect health.

Monroe decided to boldly explore the sensation. One night when the vibrations started, he realized he could move his fingers and brush them against the rug. He pressed down and his fingertips seemed to penetrate the rug. He pushed harder and his hand sank into the floor. The experience shocked him. He experimented another six times with the vibrations before he dared explore further.

Then one night, he thought about floating upward—and did. That was the beginning of his journeys into the past and future, other dimensions, even afterlife locales. He wrote three books on the subject and opened the Monroe Institute, where the phenomenon is studied and visitors learn how to leave their bodies to embark on their own journeys.

EMBARKING ON A DREAM JOURNEY

For most of us, journeys out of body are rare and spontaneous, but you can learn to "program" such experiences. Maybe you want to hover above your body, explore your neighborhood, visit a friend across town, journey to another country, or possibly another world.

The fear that you might not be able to return to your body is natural. But you don't have to worry. Getting back is the easy part. It's as if the part of you that travels is attached by a giant rubber band—you snap right back into your body when your journey ends. Perhaps you've experienced momentary OBEs, feeling a surge of power and a sense of euphoria. As soon as you realized you were out of body, the fear factor kicked in and instantly you were back in your body, awake.

Getting out—and staying out until you're ready to return—is the challenge. Because fear can hinder your efforts, it's a good idea to invoke protection before you begin. Participants at the Monroe Institute are asked to memorize this invocation:

"I deeply desire the help and cooperation, the assistance, the understanding of those individuals whose wisdom, development, and experience are equal to or greater than my own. I ask their guidance and protection from any influence or any source that might provide me with less than my stated desires."

Set a goal for your journey. Start with a modest objective, maybe hovering near the ceiling or moving around the house.

Now you're ready to slip into a relaxed state. With your eyes closed, breathe deeply, relaxing all your muscles from head to toe. As you start to drift into sleep, focus your attention on a mental object, such as a flickering candle. Once you can hold that mental state indefinitely, try maintaining your focus without concentrating on anything except the blackness in front of you.

Next, let go of your hold on the borderland of sleep and drift deeper. Give yourself a suggestion that everything you experience will be beneficial to your well-being. Repeat it several times.

Imagine two lines extending upward from the sides of your head and meeting about a foot in front of your eyes. Think of them as charged wires. Once they converge, extend them three feet from your forehead, then six feet. Shift the intersected lines 90 degrees so they extend out from the top of your head. Mentally, reach out along the lines. Keep reaching until you feel a reaction, possibly a surging, hissing, pulsating wave. Let it sweep through your entire body. At this point, you might become rigid and immobile.

Once the vibrations start, release any sense of fear, and know you can always come out of it at any time. Move the vibrations smoothly up and down around your body, in the shape of a ring. Once you've created the movement, let it continue on its own. The more rapid the movement, the easier it is to separate from your body.

Give yourself a command, such as "float upward" or "up and out." You might start out with a partial separation, exploring the area with your hand. If you're ready for a complete separation, imagine yourself lifting out and floating upward, getting lighter and lighter, enjoying the experience. Think about where you want to go. Be specific, you'll get there faster. Remember, you'll always come back.

Near-Death Experience

Near-death experiences are closely related to out-of-body experiences, except these journeys are definitely not recreational nighttime explorations. In fact, when they occur, it usually means you're temporarily dead, or very close to it.

In the summer of 1966, Jenean Gilstrap was a twenty-three-year-old mother with a newborn daughter. One night she woke up, unable to breathe. Her husband rushed her to the hospital. By the time a battery of tests had been performed, she was breathing normally. The final diagnosis was that a large gallstone had slipped out of a duct and obstructed a breathing pathway.

Shortly afterward, she went into the hospital for surgery. She remembers talking to her surgeon before she was anesthetized, then nothing more until she felt an excruciating pain in her stomach. "I remember thinking my surgeons had lied to me about the procedure. This felt as if my stomach had literally been ripped apart and a ball of fire shoved down inside it. I felt extreme coldness on the outside of my right hand, but I wasn't able to move or speak. Then I heard someone frantically say, 'She's going down! I can't get her up!' "

Jenean started rising out of her body from the top of her head, and could "see" everyone in the room, including herself, her body. "As I continued to move upward toward the ceiling, I remember looking down at myself and feeling as if the 'me of me' were being pulled away like a soft glove being slipped off." She continued to watch all the activity from the upper corner of the operating room.

At first, Jenean was frightened. She knew she was dying. "I was young and had just begun my life with my children. As I continued to have this mental dialogue with myself, I became more aware of my new surroundings and self. I focused less on my body, where the doctors were still scrambling and shouting orders. I felt surrounded by a white softness that became an all-encompassing, purely unadulterated whiteness of light."

The light called to her. She could see a silver-gray cord that connected her soul to her body. But the farther she moved from it, the greater her realization "that the thing called 'death' was not the end of anything. It was the beginning. There was nothing to fear."

She heard voices around her, relatives who had been dead for years, some of whom she had never met in the physical world. "But in this world, I knew who they were."

At the moment of complete surrender to the light, a voice asked who would raise her children. That's when she returned to her body. She was angry at the doctors for bringing her back and catapulted out again.

Jenean remembers following her body out of OR and down a hallway, where her family could see her one last time. "I could hear them plainly and was infuriated that they were making plans and arrangements for me. In that moment, I knew I was going back, that no one was going to raise my children but me."

When Jenean regained consciousness, both surgeons came to see her and told her they'd "almost lost her." She replied that they *had* lost her and related what she'd heard in the OR. They confirmed her experiences and said they'd heard of such things, but she was the first patient to ever talk about it.

For Jenean, the experience was transformational. A few months later, she woke one morning with the warmth of the sun coming through her windows and heard birds singing in a nearby tree. "I looked at myself in the bathroom mirror and realized that, at the age of twenty-three, I couldn't remember the last time I'd felt the warmth of the sun or heard birds singing. I knew I had to leave my unhappy marriage and take my children away from the unhappiness and into the warm sunshine and singing birds. I turned from the mirror, went to my closet, packed one suitcase and a diaper bag and walked out of that house, never looking back."

The Ultimate Journey

Synchronicities often occur during times of major transitions. One of those transitions is the ultimate journey we all take: death.

You've heard the stories: clocks that stop at the moment of death, the odd behavior of a pet in the days or weeks before an owner passes on, the seemingly random sighting of a crow or an owl before a loved one dies. Sometimes, plants wither and shed their petals, a garden turns brown, appliances break down for no reason, and every song you hear on the car radio is about death. You get the idea. These synchronistic occurrences can multiply when death approaches someone you love. It's as if the universe is trying to warn you and prepare you psychologically, emotionally, spiritually.

Synchronicities associated with death also manifest themselves in impulses, hunches, visions, and dreams. You might feel, for instance, the impulse to contact someone you haven't seen for a while, only to discover later that person died about the same time you were thinking of her. If, as the mystics believe, we're all connected, then information about the impending death of a loved one is available to all of us. But you have to be open to it to understand how this kind of information may come your way.

In the late 1850s, Mark Twain and his brother, Henry, worked on the Mississippi riverboats that traveled between St. Louis and New Orleans. One night while staying at their sister's home in St. Louis, Twain dreamed of his brother's corpse laid out in a metal coffin in their sister's living room. The details were specific: the coffin rested on a pair of chairs, and a bouquet with a single blood-red flower lay on Henry's chest.

Several weeks later, Twain and his brother were back in New Orleans again. This time they took different boats to St. Louis. Henry was on the *Pennsylvania*. Not far from Memphis its boilers exploded, killing numerous people. Henry was badly injured and taken to Memphis, where he died a few days later.

Most of the victims were buried in wooden coffins, but a group of Memphis women raised enough money to have Henry buried in a metal coffin, just as Twain had seen in his dream. Yet, the bouquet with that single blood-red flower was missing. While Twain stood next to his brother's body, a woman came into the room and placed a white bouquet of flowers on Henry's chest. In the center of it was a single crimson rose.

What's especially powerful about Twain's dream is that he recalled such specific details, and those details coincided precisely with the reality. His experience underscores that at a deeper level, our awareness is far greater than we realize.

The evasion of death can also be a source of potent synchronicity. On March 1, 1950, a church choir in Beatrice, Nebraska, was supposed to begin practice at 7:20 P.M. But all fifteen members of the choir were detained for perfectly legitimate and mundane reasons. The minister and his family were late because they were finishing up the laundry; another person was doing homework; yet another had car trouble. At precisely 7:25 P.M., a flaw in the heating system caused the church to explode.

This story, first reported in *Life* magazine, is one of the most extraordinary synchronistic instances of avoiding death. "If the presence of death can be the focus of such synchronistic phenomena, then it can be equally the case that the absence or avoidance of death, under certain amazing circumstances, may be just as significant and synchronistic," wrote Hopcke in *There Are No Accidents.*

It would be intriguing to know how this experience impacted the lives and beliefs of these fifteen people. Did any of them die shortly afterward? What wisdom did they take away from the experience? Were their life paths radically changed?

The death of a loved one often hurls open doors to other realities, to deeper levels of consciousness, to personal growth. Mary S is a professor in South Africa, who had never thought of herself as psychic or intuitive. "I have been an academic for more than thirty years with a PhD in literary theory, and always thought I was objective, feet firmly based on Mother Earth."

Four years ago, Mary met Danny, a psychologist. They apparently had a wonderful love affair, but because they lived 125 miles apart, it was difficult to see each other on a regular basis. So Danny asked Mary if they could shift the focus of the relationship to a more spiritual one. "He wanted us to be soul mates and to mainly 'resonate' with each other. He actually called me *La gloriosa donna della mia mente.*" The Italian phrase means the glorious lady of my mind and was what Dante called Beatrice Portinari, a woman he loved who inspired some of his writings but remained forever out of his reach. "Being a normal woman, I was a bit skeptical about just resonating. I wanted more," Mary wrote.

They communicated daily through e-mails and text messages; they exchanged poems and literary quotations. At the beginning of 2009, Mary began feeling something was wrong with Danny, that his life force was ebbing away. In February, she e-mailed him and asked if she could send him positive energy every morning at seven. He agreed, and for the next few months she did, even though she'd never done anything like this before. "It was no big deal, no flashing lights, just an 'umbilical cord' between us, with sometimes the effect of dim light around his heart."

On more than one occasion, Danny had said he would commit suicide someday, and Mary believed him. She was certain of it when he e-mailed her that his electric cables had been dug up for the fourth time by thieves, who sold the copper as scrap metal. "I just knew something terrible was going to happen." In that same e-mail, he told her he was considering taking a break for a few days, to rest.

Even though they weren't in the habit of phoning each other, Mary called him immediately. Danny was on his way home and Mary asked him where he was going. He replied that he didn't know, he just wanted to clear his head. She pleaded with him to come stay with her for a few days, because he "needed to be spoiled." He replied he might just do that.

That evening around seven, Mary texted him, asking if he had "survived the cold darkness." But his cell was turned off and the message didn't go through. She went to bed at ten, but twenty minutes later bolted upright, certain Danny needed her. She texted him again. "I am concerned about you, Love!" It didn't go through.

The next morning, Friday, Mary felt the need to meditate and send Danny energy, which she hadn't done for some time. At first, she couldn't find him, but then visualized his heart in her hands and saw a magnificent light, a pale pink shell color in the center, with bits of soft green, then a big mass of golden-cream with a clear golden halo around it. "It was so peaceful and serene, it felt holy, like total freedom and bliss, pure calm and rest. I have no words to describe it. I sat there just immersing myself in the soft energy of that light. It was as if the light was giving to me—I did not have to concentrate at all to produce it."

She sensed Danny didn't need anything, that he was calm, happy. She thought he might have gone to the Buddhist center to meditate, which would explain the light. Then she realized a light like this couldn't belong to any living being.

Saturday morning the same thing happened, but this time she sat in the presence of the light for more than an hour. It fed and comforted her. Intuitively, she felt Danny was totally at peace. "Again, I knew in my heart that no living being could produce such a light. Sunday it happened again and I got the same feeling. Also, during the whole weekend I could sense Danny's presence very strongly. It was as if he was with me, relaxed and free. I had the elated feeling of going on holiday and anticipating a long time of rest and freedom." That weekend she went into a frenzy of cooking—something Danny liked but she doesn't—with spices and ingredients he would have used.

She knew Danny wouldn't like her checking on him, so she didn't call his workplace on Monday. When she phoned Tuesday the secretary said he had died on Friday. Mary was shocked, but not surprised. She felt certain he hadn't died Friday. The police later confirmed Danny had died Thursday night between ten and eleven, the time she had sent him the last text message.

"He hanged himself in his house. It was quite clear that he had planned on doing this for a long time. Before he went, he deleted a whole life behind him. None of his friends could be contacted."

The day Mary heard about his death, a psychologist friend came to stay with her. She wanted to help Mary cope, but without infringing on her personal space. She later confided to

Mary that on that night she felt a strong presence around her, and when she left, she knew Mary was not alone.

Mary also felt this presence in the first three weeks after Danny's death—a strong, loving presence. Even though Danny's nature wasn't like this when he was alive, she felt him around her for weeks. "In his quiet manner, he was helping me through this crisis."

Mary was stunned, however, that in his will he'd left all his belongings to a friend she'd never heard of. Then she remembered he used to encourage her to be without attachment. "When I realized that nobody else had ever felt his presence after his death, I came to appreciate the wonderful farewell present he had left me: he actually came to visit me like he promised, and since then he has never really left me alone. He guided me with loving-kindness towards the realization that he had left. Nobody could phone me with the shocking account. I didn't need to identify him at the mortuary. I wasn't left with the albatross of his will and his belongings. What he gave me is the most exquisite gift anyone can receive . . . and at last I know lovers don't finally meet somewhere—they're in each other all along!"

Mary experienced synchronicity through a telepathic connection with Danny and the experience transformed her life. Perhaps she and others who report these kinds of experiences are at the leading edge of a paradigm shift. We'll explore this concept in the final chapter of this book.

Messages from the Afterlife

In dreams, our consciousness roams freely through time and space, spinning tales that have plots, characters, and motives, like a good story. Our dream stories don't always make sense, and sorting them out when we awaken can be challenging, particularly when what we remember seems like "postcards from a journey," as author Ann Faraday puts it. However, sometimes the message is clear and inspiring, especially when it comes through contact with someone who has died.

Mystics have always said we take regular nighttime journeys into reams of the afterlife that we don't remember when we wake up. Yet, dreams of contact with loved ones from the afterlife are striking. You might feel a surge of energy, as if you're more alive than usual. That's ironic, if you think contact with the deceased is dark and creepy, like a scene out of the movie *Sixth Sense*.

You may experience such a dream near the time a relative or someone close to you dies. The contact might occur spontaneously without any effort on your part. Rob knew his cousin was very ill when he appeared to Rob in a dream. To Rob's surprise, he seemed healthy and energetic, but confused. He looked around, smiling, and asked, "What's going on?" The next morning Rob received a call from his sister who told him their cousin had died.

REACHING OUT

If no such spontaneous experience occurs, you can ask to contact someone in a dream. Let's say you want to contact your grandfather, who died recently. You were close to him and have many fond memories of your times together.

As you settle into bed, relax and take a few deep breaths. Tell yourself you're about to launch a journey to make contact with your grandfather. Think of him and recall a happy time you spent together. Remember as many details as you can. Sink deeper into a meditative state as you picture yourself with your grandfather. You might tell him something about your life or your thoughts about him.

In your drowsy state, you might imagine hearing a response. Try to stay focused. See if you can continue the conversation. You might fall asleep. When you wake up, ask yourself what you dreamed. Sometimes just the effort triggers your memory.

If you can't recall any pertinent dreams, you might try this exercise as a meditation during the day. You're sending out psychic signals, and even if you don't make contact, you might encounter one or more synchronicities during the day that are directly related to memories of your grandfather.

ENGAGING THE DIVINE

"Deep down, the consciousness of mankind is one."

—DAVID BOHM, *WHOLENESS AND THE IMPLICATE ORDER*

With the expansion of the Internet in the 1990s, we entered the Information Age. Today information and nearly instantaneous communication move our civilization forward. Research that only twenty-five years ago might've taken hours, days, or weeks appears on a monitor within seconds. It seems inevitable that even synchronicity should find its way into this hi-tech Information Age.

Hi-Tech Synchronicity

One evening, a Google alert for synchronicity brought up a site called synctxt.com, a way to explore synchronicity through modern technology. The tool is described as "a research experiment and self-exploration tool that combines modern technology with the concept of synchronicity as postulated by the psychologist Carl Jung."

The technology behind the software grew out of the Princeton Anomalies Research Lab at Princeton University, where it was discovered that humans could influence quantum-scale physical events, even at a distance. This is nothing new. Physician and author Larry Dossey, for instance, explored the power of prayer (intention) in long-distance healing. Lynne McTaggart's *The Intention Experiment* explores this theory in depth. Esther and Jerry Hicks have written several books about the law of attraction that illustrate how we can influence physical events through our thoughts and intentions.

What is different, however, is that synctxt is designed for personal use. It employs random event generators (REGs) to measure the influence of consciousness on physical events and searches for patterns that indicate a deviation from expected statistical distribution. Once you sign up, a random event generator that runs 24/7 is assigned to you. When a pattern is detected, the system sends a message—written by you—to your mobile phone.

According to the website, these messages often arrive at synchronous moments. Your messages might be things like: Go with the flow. Don't worry about the small stuff. Be here now. Now you understand. Laugh. Whatever we need comes to us. Express your gratitude. Move ahead. A surprise check arrives. You're on the right track.

You might be driving to the grocery store one morning, worrying about all the bills you need to pay, when your iPhone or Blackberry jingles. At the next red light, you glance down to read a synctxt alert: Sales today, a perfect day. A couple of hours later, the mail arrives and with it a check for a sizable amount, a refund you'd forgotten about.

Another afternoon, you're on the phone, talking with a friend about an upcoming event you two are organizing for a charity. You're both getting frustrated by all the details. That's when an alert comes through: Trust the process.

These messages qualify as synchronicities. In fact, the one about money was a premonition. But by a machine? Not exactly. Although the message is transmitted digitally and the generator is a machine, you created the messages.

On the website, some users have shared their stories. One of the most striking proved synctxt works even for people who haven't subscribed to the service. A subscriber had created a message that said, "See? All it takes is time." A few days later she was in a bar with a friend, who was discussing her plans to become an independent architect. But she was worried about how long it would take. She finished her story by remarking that if she stuck with it, she could probably have her own practice by the time she was thirty. As soon as she said this, her friend got a text on her phone that said, See? All it takes is time! "She was pretty impressed, and I think it made her feel a little better and more confident about her plans."

As more people connect to the underlying reality of synchronicity, a window opens with a view into the next age, one of transformation. By actively engaging synchronicity and trusting our subconscious selves, we begin to live more consciously, more thoughtfully. We grasp the interconnectedness of all life and fully understand that what affects one affects all.

The Transformation Age

In this age, answers can come to you as if by magic. You know who you are and who you wish to become. You're in the right place at the right time. Synchronicity is your best friend and its messages act as your compass. In the Transformation Age, you easily bring your focus to your intentions and desires, and invite synchronicity into your life. In the Transformation Age, you engage the divine.

That's the ideal. But to get to that place, you must learn how to ask your questions, define your desires, and frame your life so you create a rich environment in which synchronicities can readily occur. In such an environment, the law of attraction works as never before; intuition deepens, creativity flourishes. "Once you decide to work with coincidence, you invite new energy patterns into your life," wrote Robert Moss in *The Three "Only" Things*. "You not only observe events in a new way; you actually draw events and people toward you in a way that is different from before." Everything in your life starts shifting in a richer, more positive direction.

Synchronicities, when you're aware of them, are like whispered cues, signposts along life's road. Take this turn, go straight here. Take a risk. Slow down, speed up. In the Transformation Age, if you're a part of it, synchronicities happen every day. Yet, they aren't everyday experiences.

Not everyone has a computer in the Information Age, and not everyone will be following the synchronistic path in the Transformation Age. But the influences will be felt universally.

Deepak Chopra identifies two states of higher awareness: divine consciousness and unity consciousness. In the first, our ability to manifest desires increases. The divine consciousness, an experience that comes and goes, allows us to glimpse the "presence of Spirit in all things" as Mary S did after the suicide of her lover, described in the previous chapter. Unity consciousness or enlightenment involves "the complete transformation of the personal self into the universal self, a state in which miracles happen and all is possible." Can we engage the divine, even for brief moments?

The Law of Attraction

Metaphysicians have been writing about the law of attraction since before the printing press was invented. But it was first popularized in the twentieth century by author Jane Roberts.

In the fall of 1963, Jane Roberts began to channel Seth, "a personality essence no longer focused in physical reality." Jane's husband, Robert Butts, recognized the quality of the Seth material and began taking notes during her trance sessions. By the time Jane died in 1984, there were more than twenty Seth books and hundreds of unpublished notebooks on a vast spectrum of topics—the nature of physical reality, life after death, reincarnation, health and illness, human and animal intelligence, the nature of consciousness, war and peace, and politics. The cornerstone of Seth's philosophy was simple: "You create your reality; you get what you concentrate on . . . there is no other main rule."

In other words, the law of attraction. Many of Seth's descriptions about the nature of reality echo the contentions of David Bohm and other scientists—about how everything in the universe is connected and the importance of intent and belief in creating our experiences. According to Seth, "Because beliefs form reality—the structure of experience—any change in beliefs altering that structure initiates change . . . ."

The Seth books provide a philosophical basis for the nature of reality and consciousness, the law of attraction, and the role of beliefs in creating our realities. However, they may have been lacking in practical application. Just how do you do this? Fortunately, other authors (we've mentioned some of them in this book) have presented the law of attraction in ways that make it accessible to millions. Common themes run through their books: the importance of beliefs, focused intense desire, and powerful emotions.

In the following two stories, you'll see the importance of beliefs, intense desire, and strong emotions.

For Jane Clifford, a single mother in Wales, her consuming desire and focused intention brought about the results she needed. Her youngest son, Harry, wasn't thriving in the local secondary school and had asked if he could attend an expensive private school where his older brother had completed his education. Harry wasn't a scholar, but he was a brilliant musician and the school agreed to interview him on that basis.

The interview went so well that the headmaster decided to create a place for Harry and gave Jane maximum funding. But even with the funding, she still needed £8,000 a year for two years and another £32,000 to complete his education. Her relationship with Harry's dad had ended, her debts had piled up, she had no means of support. She didn't even have anything left to sell.

Various friends and family members invested in Harry, and Jane scraped together what she could, when she could. But that £32,000 loomed in front of her, a seemingly insurmountable obstacle. While in London, a good friend told her to visit a tiny church where there were shrines to St. Anthony (saint of lost things) and St. Jude (saint of lost causes). Her friend had been to the church years earlier but could recall only the general location. With just a vague description, Jane set out to find the little church.

She asked every London cab driver outside the tube station about the location of the church; she inquired in cafes and shops, but to no avail. Discouraged and frustrated, she nearly gave up. "I decided to buy a peach from a stall holder. I asked him if he knew where this little church was and he pointed across the street."

Jane hurried inside the church, lit a candle, and thanked St. Anthony for all his help with lost car keys over the years. Then she lit a candle to St. Jude and asked him for help with the school fees. For the next three months, with no solution in sight, she remained anxious and unsettled.

During a reunion of classmates at the school, Harry volunteered to help at dinner. An elderly gentleman engaged Harry in conversation and said he understood Harry might not be able to continue attending the school. Harry explained that his mother couldn't afford it. The old gent said, "I shouldn't worry about that if I were you, Harry," then turned away to speak to a dinner guest.

It turned out the gentleman was making a considerable financial gift to the school that very day. The money was to be invested, the interest used to help poorer students. "He specified that only in Harry's case could some capital be used to pay all of Harry's remaining fees to enable him to finish his education there!" Jane wrote. "Miracle!"

Jane not only had a powerful desire and intention, she refused to give up. Even though no one seemed to know the location of the little church, she kept asking and finally found it. It was exactly the synchronicity she needed. She literally engaged the divine by visiting the shrines of the two saints and requesting help.

HARNESSING SYNCHRONICITY

See if you can put synchronicity to work for you. Think of a question. Or, focus on a goal. Make it something meaningful. Be serious. Be passionate. Back it with powerful emotion. What do you really want or really need? If you're having trouble formulating a question or setting a goal, find a quiet space and relax. Let your mind wander as you get settled, telling yourself that the most important question for you at this time will come to mind. Let go of extraneous thoughts. Watch for the issue and the question. When it comes to you, refine it. Make it specific, yet simple.

Expect results. Imagine that you've already received your answer. How does it feel? What are you doing differently now that you've got your answer? Write it down, tell your friends. Put the word out to the universe.

Set a time frame for getting an answer. You might try an all-or-nothing approach by telling yourself the next thing you hear—a voice on television, a comment in a shop or parking lot—will provide an answer. That might work best for those of you who are intuitive and frequently notice synchronicities. Maybe you'll want to give yourself a day or two for the message to appear. If you don't recognize it, focus again and begin anew.

Look for something unusual in your environment, something unexpected. Maybe it's a call from someone you haven't talked to for a long time. Or a chance meeting with someone. Any unexpected encounter could provide a forum for obtaining your answer. What's the first thing the person says to you? Can you find a meaning related to your question or goal? Does it offer you direction, a new approach, or maybe a warning? If you're not certain, watch for the next synchronicity while you keep thinking about your question or goal.

With practice, it will become easier for you to harness synchronicity by creating space in your mind and your heart for it to manifest itself. Some people, like Jane, use prayer, visualization, and ritual. Others follow the environmental cues, as Jennifer Gerard did in her trip to China and Nepal, which changed her life. Perhaps, during your exploration of synchronicity, your intuitive voice has grown sufficiently strong so that you listen to it more closely. Maybe you now follow your impulses, search for messages in your dreams, read the events you experience as symbolic of your intentions and beliefs.

If, at this point in your journey, you're still uncertain of your intentions and beliefs, then look around you. Everything you see in your personal life—family, home, loved ones, pets, children and partners, career triumphs and losses, your health and prosperity—is a result of intentions and beliefs you hold, desires you have. If you see elements you dislike, change your beliefs. Your experiences and external reality will change accordingly.

Leah Southey, a writer and editor, has a guardian angel, Shiva, who helps her whenever she's in a tough spot. In March 2007, she and her husband, Neil, visited Jenolan Caves in Australia, where they celebrated their wedding anniversary. They were on a day tour of the caves when her husband realized his keys were missing. They didn't know how they would get home again. Leah asked Neil if he wanted to find the keys himself or if he wanted someone to hand them to him. For Leah, this part of the decision—the intention—was the most important element.

"We agreed someone bringing them to us would be better. Despite that, he insisted we retrace our steps, go to the kiosk and the National Parks office to see if anyone had handed them in. When that failed, he went on a second tour of the cave we had already seen."

While he was doing that, Leah sat by the river and asked Shiva where the keys were. "In a crisis, I automatically go to Shiva. He has helped me many times." The answer? The keys were at the cave entrance.

When she and Neil met up again, they returned to the cave entrance but didn't find the keys. "The tourist area was about to close when a couple of park officers drove around the parking area. They stopped next to us and a woman asked, 'Would these help?' She was dangling our keys out the window."

The couple not only got their keys back, they got them in the way they had requested: someone handed them over. When

Leah asked where the keys had been found, the woman said, "At the cave entrance."

By requesting help from Shiva, by believing the keys would be found, by defining their intention, Leah and her husband activated the law of attraction and engaged the divine.

The Way of Luck

In the previous chapter, we told the story of the church choir in Beatrice, Nebraska, whose members were all late for practice the evening the church blew up. Lucky people, right? So what's the difference between synchronicity and luck, and how can we harness it?

In essence, good luck is a fortunate synchronicity. But it doesn't happen on its own. It usually takes some sort of action. Imagine dreaming six numbers that turn out to be the winning digits for the Powerball lottery the next day. That's synchronicity. However, it would only be luck if you acted on your dream and bought a ticket using those numbers. In the case of the church choir, the members' action was inaction, or delayed action.

When someone becomes an overnight success, we call that person lucky. But a closer look usually reveals that the "sudden" success followed years, even decades, of effort. Elmore Leonard wrote thirty-seven novels before he hit upon the genre that made him famous: mystery and crime. Harrison Ford got bits parts and worked as a carpenter until he found success acting in George Lucas's movie *American Graffiti* in 1973. Stephen King tossed out his manuscript for *Carrie*, but his wife retrieved it from the trash; the paperback rights eventually sold for $400,000 and launched King's career. Jeff Lindsay wrote in various genres over the years, but he was in his mid-fifties when he hit success with a character named Dexter. There are now five books in the series, the latest a *New York Times* bestseller, and Dexter is Showtime's highest-rated program.

After graduating from college, Trish wrote five novels before writing the one that got published. Some would say she was lucky, because her work was selected from hundreds, even thousands, of manuscripts written by competent writers. But it wasn't just luck, it took work, strong intent, and the guidance of synchronicities. The editor at Ballantine Books, who bought the manuscript, read it the weekend after he watched the premiere of *Miami Vice*. Like the television show, *In Shadow* featured two Miami detectives, one white, one black, who were involved in a drug investigation. Synchronicity. The editor made an offer the following Monday and Trish's fiction-writing career was launched. The interest came with the twenty-fifth submission of her sixth novel, the first and only one of those six novels to be published.

Rob had studied anthropology in college and traveled the world to visit archaeological sites between jobs in journalism. But when he was hired to write what would become the first of eight Indiana Jones novels, neither LucasFilm nor the editor at Bantam Books knew of his interest in archaeology. They only knew he'd published one novel, *Crystal Skull*.

When we are focused, passionate, pushing our limits, our brains release endorphins. Research indicates this happens during sex and childbirth, strenuous exercise, meditation, and intense creative work. If you visualize what you want when endorphins are rushing through you, desires manifest more quickly. It's as if the endorphins somehow help connect you to the powerful source of who you really are and the potential of who you can become.

"A serendipitous cosmos is a playful, childlike one, and an adventurous and joyful approach to life encourages synchronicity," wrote Marcus Anthony, author of *Sage of Synchronicity*. "A key point is bringing the mind fully into the present moment. In the joyful state of complete presence, it is as if the cosmos comes alive. The deeper meaning and purpose of things becomes known even as they unfold, as if your psyche and the cosmic mind are in open dialogue."

As synchronicities occur, it's important to ask what they mean. The answer might come in the form of another synchronicity. You might catch a certain song on the radio, hear something said on TV, or read a passage in a book. The more you explore synchronicity, the greater your understanding becomes. The less resistance you have to such experiences, the more likely it is you'll attract more of them. Lack of resistance is a major component in the law of attraction.

When the meaning doesn't jump out at you, look at synchronicities as opportunities, especially for exploring creative alternatives. Then you're attracting luck. As Patricia Einstein wrote in *Intuition: The Path to Inner Wisdom*, "We've all had the experience of being in the right place at the right time, and at some point in our lives we've all known someone whom we characterized as lucky. Luck . . . is not a matter of chance. It's really a question of synchronicity."

Here's one final story, an astonishing one that combines synchronicity, belief and intention, and personal transformation.

Oprah Is Calling

In 1988, Carol Bowman's young son sat on her lap and related his past-life memories as a Civil War soldier. As a result of his recollection, her son's terror of loud noises and a chronic health problem vanished. Nothing in her life up to that point had aroused her curiosity to such a high pitch. She became obsessed with learning what she could about these memories in children. She began her informal "research" of children's past-life memories, interviewed parents she knew, scoured bookstores and libraries for books on reincarnation and past lives.

Carol found some academic works about children's past lives but quickly realized no one had written a practical book for parents that explained what to do if your child expressed a past-life memory. She realized she should write that book. "I didn't stop to consider the fact that I hadn't written anything longer than a term paper in college. I knew I had to do it, and somehow I would."

By January of 1992, she'd collected some case studies from parents whose children had past-life memories and the book was taking shape in her head. She and a friend went to a past-life conference in Florida so Carol could meet and network with people in the field. During a presentation by bestselling author and physician Brian Weiss, he mentioned that he'd been on Oprah. "As soon as he said it, everything seemed to fall away around me," Carol recalled. "I felt a bolt of energy race through my body and with a certain, deep knowing I heard in my inner mind, *You will be on Oprah, too*. I immediately turned to my friend and whispered, 'I'm going to be on Oprah, too.'" Her friend thought she was joking and laughed.

As part of her strategy to legitimize her research and add credibility to her work, Carol enrolled in a graduate program in counseling at Villanova University. She was due to start school the same week that her husband, Steve, learned he was being downsized from his corporate job. It was a shock, but Carol figured that now, more than ever, she needed to pursue her dream. She assumed Steve would soon find another job and things would return to normal.

Instead, things went from bad to worse. Doors kept closing for Steve—they had no steady income. Steve began doing freelance business writing to generate income. "But starting a business takes time and with two children and a mortgage, we didn't have the luxury of time."

Carol continued with her research, gathering stories from parents she met at school functions and on playgrounds. One mother, Colleen, had a young son who experienced traumatic nightmares that Carol recognized as past-life memories. She helped the boy. Colleen was so impressed she said she was writing Oprah about Carol's research.

Great, Carol thought. But that didn't pay the family's mounting credit card debt. By 1994, she and Steve worried that they might not be able to stay in their home, a heartbreaking prospect. They couldn't bear to tell their kids they were considering selling the house. Even though she was in graduate school, the pressure was on. Carol started looking for full-time work.

"I hadn't had a real job in ten years, my computer skills were minimal. I was so desperate that I applied for a sales job with Scott Paper, but they wouldn't even hire me to sell toilet paper. That was a low moment. My self-esteem was really in the toilet." Even more troubling was that Carol felt she had something valuable to offer the world. She held stubbornly to her dream but kept hitting insurmountable obstacles. As each month passed, the dream seemed to slip a little farther away from her.

Carol didn't give up, but things didn't improve, either. One particularly bleak, bitingly cold day in February 1994, she walked through her neighborhood, raging at the universe.

"Okay, if you want me to write a book, help me!" she shouted at the unseen forces around her. "With tears streaming down my face, I gave the universe an ultimatum. I felt like a jerk, but I was angry at the unfairness of it all."

She was so ashamed of her behavior that when she arrived home, she sat on the front porch, unable to go inside. Steve poked his head out the door, his face seized with shock, and handed her the phone. "Listen to the message," he said. A woman spoke. "This is *The Oprah Winfrey Show* calling for Carol Bowman. Could you please call me back?"

"In that moment, I knew my prayers were answered. Within a week, my kids and I, along with other mothers, were in Chicago talking to Oprah about our children's past-life memories. She devoted a whole show to my research. I reasoned that if Oprah was interested in my work, surely others would be."

Curiously, when Oprah's office received Colleen's letter, it had been misfiled under children's phobias. Apparently they wanted to do a show on children's past-life memories but couldn't find an expert. Synchronistically, the delay worked to Carol's benefit. It gave her a year to collect cases.

When she returned from Chicago, Carol began contacting authors she knew about her book idea and asked how to find a literary agent. With the Oprah show behind her, she felt someone would finally pay attention to what she had to offer. A successful author in her field recommended his literary agent, and Carol and Steve met with her in New York. For the next few months, Carol and Steve worked full time writing a hundred-page proposal. "Again, this meant we weren't generating any income. We were operating on pure faith. After all, if Oprah called, this would certainly happen, too."

They finished the proposal. Weeks passed. Then months. Carol realized the agent wasn't doing anything and contacted other agents. Some openly laughed at her for thinking anyone would be interested in such a topic. Others wouldn't talk to her until she got out of the contract with the first agent.

A friend with connections in publishing had offered help months before, so Carol called her and explained the situation. "Her husband made a phone call and said that Ian Ballantine, the founder of Ballantine and Bantam Books, would like to look at my proposal. I didn't know anything about publishing, or who Ian Ballantine was, but I was grateful that someone was willing to look at it."

Within a few weeks, Ian, then seventy-nine years old, called and said he would like to help her get the book published. He offered to introduce Carol to the CEOs of some publishing houses, most of whom he had trained. "I actually screamed when I got off the phone. Steve came running upstairs to find me jumping up and down, screaming. Another miracle!"

Ian and Betty Ballantine, his wife and publishing partner, met Carol and Steve in New York and set up a meeting with Irwyn Appelbaum, president of Bantam Books. After a two-hour meeting, Appelbaum asked Carol what she wanted. "I told him to make me an offer. Steve's jaw dropped by my uncharacteristic bargaining strategy. But at this point, I had a six-digit number in mind that we needed to pay down our substantial credit card debt, create an office space in the house where I could write, and sustain us for the time it would take for Steve and me to finish the book. I had gotten this far, why not dream on?"

Appelbaum called her at home and offered a substantial advance. Carol countered by doubling it. "I knew I was taking a risk, but I also knew what we needed to get out of trouble. There was a moment of silence, then Irwyn accepted my counter offer. I collapsed in a heap of relief."

Before the contract was signed, Steve and Carol met the Ballantines in New York again for a celebratory lunch. The very next day, Carol got a call from Betty, telling her that Ian had died. "We were devastated. My new friend and mentor had vanished almost as quickly as he had appeared."

Betty edited the book, and Carol is eternally grateful to her and her husband for giving her a start in publishing. "These invisible forces, the good fortune, the synchronicities, orchestrated and propelled me on this journey."

When we heard this story, we could hardly believe it. It sounded like a corny plot element in a movie: first-time writer with no agent is offered a substantial advance, then negotiates with the president of a major publishing house and convinces him to double a six-figure offer. That kind of thing doesn't happen in real life. But it did. Carol followed the synchronistic clues, refused to surrender her dream, had an unshakeable belief that she had something unique to offer, and kept moving forward on nothing more than faith, that unity of consciousness. And she found her life's work.

FINE-TUNING YOUR INTUITION

When Carol Bowman asked the universe how she could get her book published, the answer came in a very big and obvious way with a call from *The Oprah Winfrey Show*. What could be more direct than a call from the person with a track record for creating bestsellers?

Of course, not all answers come in such a straightforward manner. Sometimes they need interpretation, as we've talked about in other chapters. And sometimes, you have to wait until the meaning becomes clear.

Write down one of your burning desires. Be passionate about it, descriptive; imagine how this desire may manifest itself in your life.

You've just answered the question you jotted down at the end of Secret 1!

CONCLUSION

Once you begin to experience synchronicity on a regular basis, your life shifts into a deeper, richer realm. It's easier to attract the people, opportunities, and situations that benefit you. You feel you're on track, in the groove, firmly grounded in the moment, exactly where you're meant to be.

Esther and Jerry Hicks call this state "being in alignment with source." Eckhart Tolle calls it "the power of now." Deepak Chopra refers to it as "divine consciousness." Regardless of what name you give it, the bottom line is that your consciousness has been transformed. You're now able to experience the life and relationships you imagine.

RESOURCES

Anthony, Marcus. *Sage of Synchronicity: Creating and Living Your Bliss Using Integrated Intelligence*. Hong Kong: Benjamin Franklin Press Asia, 2010.

Bair, Deirdre. *Jung: A Biography*. New York: Little, Brown, 2003.

Belitz, Charlene and Lundstrom, Meg. *The Power of Flow: Practical Ways to Transform Your Life with Meaningful Coincidence*. New York: Random House, 1997.

Cameron, Julia. *The Artist's Way: A Spiritual Path to Higher Creativity*. New York: Jeremy P. Tarcher/Putnam, 1992.

Chopra, Deepak. *The Spontaneous Fulfillment of Desire: Harnessing the Infinite Power of Coincidence*. New York: Harmony Books, 2003.

Combs, Allan, and Holland, Mark. *Synchronicity: Science, Myth, and the Trickster*. New York: Marlowe & Company, 1989.

Graff, Dale E. *Tracks in the Psychic Wilderness: An Exploration of Remote Viewing, ESP, Precognitive Dreaming, and Synchronicity*. Shaftesbury, Dorset and Boston: Element Books, 1998.

Grasse, Ray. *The Waking Dream: Unlocking the Symbolic Language of Our Lives*. Wheaten, Ill.: Theosophical Publishing House/Quest Books, 1996.

Hopcke, Robert. H. *There Are No Accidents: Synchronicity and the Stories of Our Lives*. New York: Riverhead Books, 1997.

Jones, Roger S. *Physics as Metaphor*. New York: Plume Books, 1983.

Joseph, Frank. *Synchronicity & You: Understanding the Role of Meaningful Coincidence in Your Life*. Shaftesbury, Dorset and Boston: Element Books, 1999.

Jung, C. G. *Memories, Dreams, Reflections*. Translated by Richard Winston and Clara Winston. New York: Vintage Books, 1961.

Jung, C. G. *Synchronicity: An Acausal Connecting Principle*. Translated by R. F. C. Hull. Princeton, N. J.: Princeton University Press, 1969.

Koestler, Arthur. *The Roots of Coincidence: An Excursion into Parapsychology*. New York: Vintage Books, 1972.

MacGregor, Rob. *Dream Power for Teens*. Avon, Mass.: Adams Media, 2005.

MacGregor, Rob. *Psychic Power: Discover and Develop Your Sixth Sense at Any Age*. Hauppauge, N.Y.: Barron's Educational Services, 2005.

MacGregor, Rob and Grosso, Tony. *The Rainbow Oracle: The Book of Color Divination*. New York: Ballantine Books, 1989.

MacGregor, Trish and Gemondo, Millie. *Animal Totems: The Power and Prophecy of Your Animal Guides*. Gloucester, Mass.: Fair Winds Press, 2004.

Mansfield, Victor. *Synchronicity, Science, and Soul-Making: Understanding Jungian Synchronicity Through Physics, Buddhism, and Philosophy*. Peru, Ill: Open Court Publishing Company, 1995.

Marshall, Richard and others, *Mysteries of the Unexplained*. Pleasantville, NY: Reader's Digest Books, 1982.

McKenna, Dennis J. and McKenna, Terence K. *The Invisible Landscape: Mind, Hallucinogens, and the I Ching*. New York: HarperCollins, 1993.

McTaggart, Lynne. *The Intention Experiment: Using Your Thoughts to Change Your Life and Your World.* New York: Free Press/Simon & Schuster, 2007.

Monroe, Robert A. *Journeys Out of the Body.* New York: Broadway Books, 1977.

Moss, Robert. *Conscious Dreaming: A Spiritual Path for Everyday Life.* New York: Three Rivers Press, 1996.

Moss, Robert. *The Three "Only" Things: Tapping the Power of Dreams, Coincidence & Imagination.* Novato, Calif.: New World Library, 2007.

Peat, F. David. *Synchronicity: The Bridge Between Matter and Mind.* New York: Bantam Books, 1987.

Pinchbeck, Daniel. *2012: The Return of Quetzalcoatl.* New York: Jeremy P. Tarcher/Penquin, 2006.

Roberts, Jane. *The Unknown Reality: A Seth Book.* Englewood Cliffs, N.J.: Prentice-Hall Press, 1977.

Sheldrake, Rupert. *Dogs That Know When Their Owners Are Coming Home: And Other Unexplained Powers of Animals.* New York: Crown Publishers, 1999.

Shultz, Mona Lisa, MD, PhD. *Awakening Intuition: Using Your Mind-Body Network for Insight and Healing*. New York: Harmony Books, 1998.

Skafte, Dianne. *Listening to the Oracle: The Ancient Art of Finding Guidance in the Signs and Symbols All Around Us*. San Francisco: HarperSanFrancisco, 1997.

Storm, Lance, Ed. *Synchronicity: Multiple Perspectives on Meaningful Coincidence*. Pari, Italy: Pari Publishing, 2008.

Tarnas, Richard. *Cosmos and Psyche: Intimations of a New World View*. New York: Plume, 2007.

Vaughan, Alan. *Patterns of Prophecy*. New York: Dell Publishing, 1973.

Vaughan, Alan. *Incredible Coincidence: The Baffling World of Synchronicity*. New York: Ballantine Signet, 1980.

Wilson, Colin. *C. G. Jung: Lord of the Underworld*. London: Aeon, 2005.

INDEX

HAY HOUSE TITLES OF RELATED INTEREST

THE POWER OF CONTAGIOUS THINKING: How Your Thoughts Can Influence the World,
by David R. Hamilton PhD

ALONG THE PATH TO ENLIGHTENMENT: 365 Daily Reflections from Dr David Hawkins,
by David R. Hawkins PhD, MD

THE BIOLOGY OF BELIEF: Unleashing the Power of Consciousness, Matter & Miracles, by Bruce Lipton PhD

COSMIC ORDERING FOR BEGINNERS, by Barbel Mohr

THE POWER OF INTENTION: Learning to Co-create Your World Your Way, by Dr Wayne W. Dyer

SPONTANEOUS EVOLUTION: Our Positive Future and a Way to Get There from Here,
by Bruce H. Lipton & Steve Bhaerman

All the above are available at your local bookshop,
or can be ordered via www.hayhouse.co.uk

ABOUT THE AUTHORS

Rob and Trish MacGregor, professional writers for twenty-five years, have mined numerous synchronicities and fruitfully used the knowledge derived from them. A synchronistic meeting on a flight in the 1980s, for example, resulted in their leading adventure tours to South America for Avianca Airlines. One synchronicity after another led to their many nonfiction books n dreams, psychic development, astrology, yoga, the tarot, divination, nd animal symbolism. In 2003, they took over the writing of the popular ydney Omarr astrology series.

They are also award-winning novelists. Rob has written seven Indiana Jones novels, which have sold millions of copies. He won the coveted dgar Allan Poe Award for *Prophecy Rock*, and its sequel, *Hawk Moon*, ras an Edgar finalist. Trish, writing as T. J. MacGregor, won the Edgar

in 2003 for best original paperback, for *Out of Sight*. Her thirty novels and books have been translated into fourteen languages. The most recent, *Esperanza*—written as Trish J. MacGregor—was published in September 2010.

They have one daughter, Megan, an art major and an aspiring writer. They live in South Florida with three cats and a golden retriever.

www.robmacgregor.net
www.tjmacgregor.com

JOIN THE HAY HOUSE FAMILY

As the leading self-help, mind, body and spirit publisher in the UK, we'd like to welcome you to our family so that you can enjo all the benefits our website has to offer.

 EXTRACTS from a selection of your favourite author titles

 COMPETITIONS PRIZES & SPEC OFFERS Win extracts, money off, downloads and so much m

 **LISTEN** to a range of radio interviews and our latest audio publications

 CELEBRATE YO BIRTHDAY An inspiring gift w be sent your w

 **LATEST NEWS** Keep up with the latest news from and about our authors

 ATTEND OUR AUTHOR EVEN Be the first to hear about ou author events

 **iPHONE APPS** Download your favourite app for your iPhone

 **HAY HOUSE INFORMATION** Ask us anythi all enquiries answered

join us online at w   use.co.

 292B Kensal Road
T: 020 8962 1230 E: uk